1676 PROJECT

HOW NEW JERSEY SHAPED AMERICA

1676 PROJECT

HOW NEW JERSEY SHAPED AMERICA

SETH GROSSMAN

1676 PROJECT

How New Jersey Shaped America

Publisher:
Seth Grossman,
453 Shore Road, Somers Point, NJ 08244 USA.

ISBN 979-8-9944490-1-1

Library of Congress Control Number: 2026907123

Funding has been made possible in part by the New Jersey Historical Commission, a division of Cultural Affairs within the Department of State, through funds administered by the Atlantic County Office of Cultural and Heritage Affairs.

Typesetting and book cover design:
Joanna & Grzegorz Japoł – LUNA Design Studio

Introduction

Most of today's schools and colleges use the basic narrative of "The 1619 Project" to teach American history. That "project" is a collection of teaching materials that has been published and distributed by The New York Times Magazine since 2019.

Its premise is that the traditional values, culture, and institutions of America were shaped by what happened in Jamestown, Virginia, in 1619. That was when black Africans were first sold there as slaves. It suggests that America needed a "fundamental transformation" during the past fifty years because it was built on slavery, conquest, and exploitation. That narrative is deceptive and inaccurate.

This book presents an honest and complete history. It describes how America was instead shaped by Quakers who created what is now known as South Jersey in 1676.

It begins with Native Americans migrating to South Jersey at the end of the Ice Age. It describes important events in the Middle East that brought Italian merchant sailors to the Atlantic Ocean, and then to America. It explains how "Wars of Religion" between Muslims and Christians, and then Catholics and Protestants, brought the English to Virginia and Massachusetts.

It then tells the remarkable story of George Fox. During the turmoil and violence of the English Civil Wars, this 23-year-old began preaching a new and radical Christian doctrine of peace, equality, and simplicity. Within a few years, he had more than 50,000 followers. They called themselves "The Religious Society of Friends." Their detractors called them Quakers. They were often persecuted and jailed.

"George Fox Preaching in a Tavern in England in 1650" Watercolor by Edward Henry Wehnert (1865), Public Domain.

In 1674, those Quakers seized an opportunity to buy a half-interest in New Jersey, a failing British colony in North America. In 1676, they persuaded their co-owner to divide it into two separate colonies. The Quakers then owned and controlled most of what is now known as South Jersey. They wanted it to be more than a mere refuge. They wanted it to be a place where Quakers could put their vision for a better world into practice. There they could "show its strengths to the world."

In 1676, those Quakers drafted and adopted a written charter that served as a constitution. It had an elected Assembly, secret ballots, and a comprehensive "Bill of Rights."

They then created counties, towns, and townships with frugal governments that provided only the services they needed. They had few laws and officials, and almost no taxes. Yet people were free and safe, and their property was protected. Disputes were quickly and peacefully settled. Children were educated.

Most people in Quaker New Jersey soon produced far more than they needed. Their governments let them keep and enjoy almost all of it.

This made South Jersey a "poor man's paradise." Most settlers arrived as indentured servants with nothing but debt. Yet within ten years, most were comfortable, if not wealthy.

Quakers were taught and expected to live by the "Golden Rule." They were to equally offer all others the rights and opportunities they enjoyed. There were no wars with Native Americans in South Jersey. There was no "Trail of Tears." Women and Blacks could vote there in 1776. A handful of Quakers shamed most slave owners in South Jersey into freeing their slaves before American independence.

Five years after 1676, William Penn established a second "Quaker Commonwealth" in Pennsylvania. Both Quaker colonies became lands of "Liberty and Prosperity" long before those words became the motto of New Jersey.

During the 1730s, there was a revival of Christian faith throughout British North America. Preachers from many denominations traveled in all thirteen colonies. They inspired and energized large crowds wherever they went. They made Christian faith and Bible values part of day-to-day American life.

Courthouse in Salem, New Jersey built in 1735. Photograph posted to Wikimedia Commons and released into the Public Domain by "Smallbones" in 2010.

This revival became known as "The Great Awakening." It connected Quaker South Jersey and Philadelphia with the other British colonies in many ways. It made them all part of one new American nation of "Liberty and Prosperity."

This book invites every school and college in America to use a "1676 Project" to teach this to the next generation.

Atlantic City, New Jersey. January 1, 2026

Table of contents

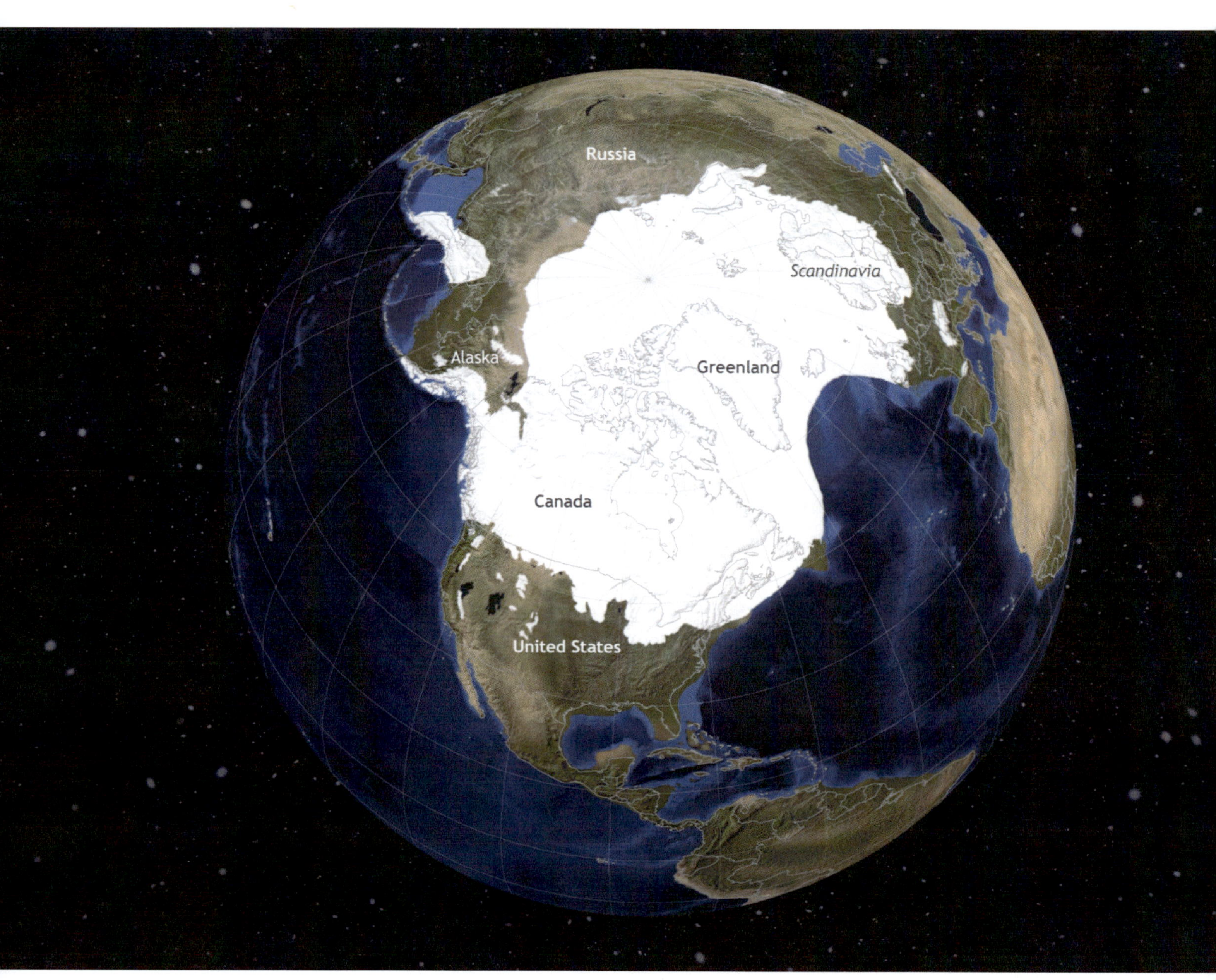

A Map Depicting the Ice Sheets That Covered Much of North America during the peak of the last Ice Age, approximately 20,000 Years Ago. Source. National Oceanic and Atmospheric Administration (NOAA), Climate.gov. Public Domain.

1.

An Ice Age creates a land bridge from Asia. Native Americans migrate to America.

Between 19,000 and 26,000 years ago, the Earth became much colder than it is today. In northern Europe, Asia, and North America, snow that fell during winter did not melt in the summer. For thousands of years, the snow piled up and was compressed into thick sheets of moving ice called glaciers. What are now Canada and the northern parts of the United States, including northern New Jersey, were covered with ice. The ice over what is now Chicago was roughly 3,000 feet thick.

Those giant glaciers contained so much frozen water that sea levels were 400 feet below what they are today. What is now Atlantic City was 30 to 50 miles away from the ocean. Dry land connected eastern Asia and western North America. Geologists call it the "Bering Land Bridge" or "Beringia."

During that time, groups of Asians living in what are now Mongolia and Siberia migrated to North America and settled here. Their descendants are now called American Indians or Native Americans.

At this time, it is not known whether they walked along ice-free sections of the landbridge or whether they used boats to paddle or sail along the coast.

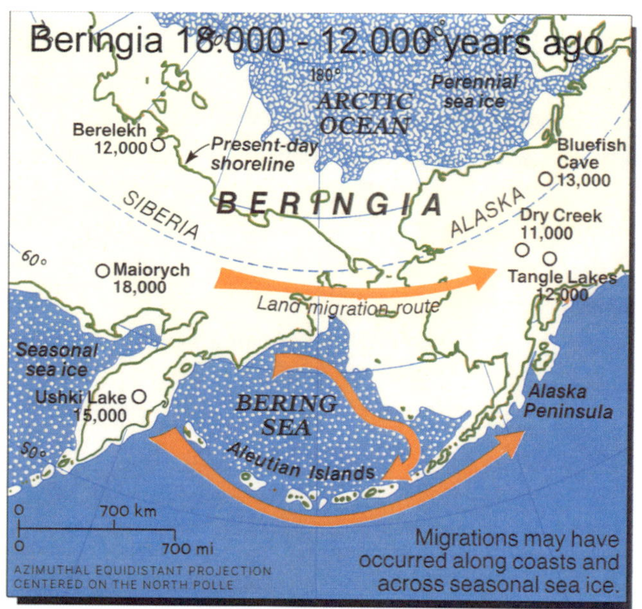

Map of Beringia Land Bridge 18,000 to 12,000 Years Ago by Thinkquest. (Most scientists now believe that this Landbridge existed 19,000 to 26,000 years ago and that the migration took place then.)

Artist's depiction of "The First People" crossing the Beringian Landbridge from what is now Siberia to what is now Alaska during the Ice Age. From a 2021 post by Michelle Freson in Ancient Origins.

2.

Algonquians (Algonkians) and Iroquois move Northeast as the earth warms.

About 13,000 years ago, the earth slowly warmed and the giant glaciers melted. Most of their water flowed into the oceans and raised sea levels to close to what they are today. Water from these melting glaciers also created thousands of lakes throughout Canada and the northern United States. They include the five Great Lakes in the Midwest, and Lake Hopatcong in New Jersey. *(In 1831, Lake Hopatcong was made deeper and wider with a dam that supplied water to the Morris Canal.)*

As the earth warmed, two large groups of Native Americans moved to what are now the northeast United States and Quebec and Ontario in Canada.

The largest group were the Algonquians (also Algonkians). They included the Powhatan of Virginia, the Mahican and Massachusett of New England, the Shawnee of Ohio, and the Algonquian of Quebec and Ontario. Pocahontas was a Powhatan who spoke an Algonquian dialect.

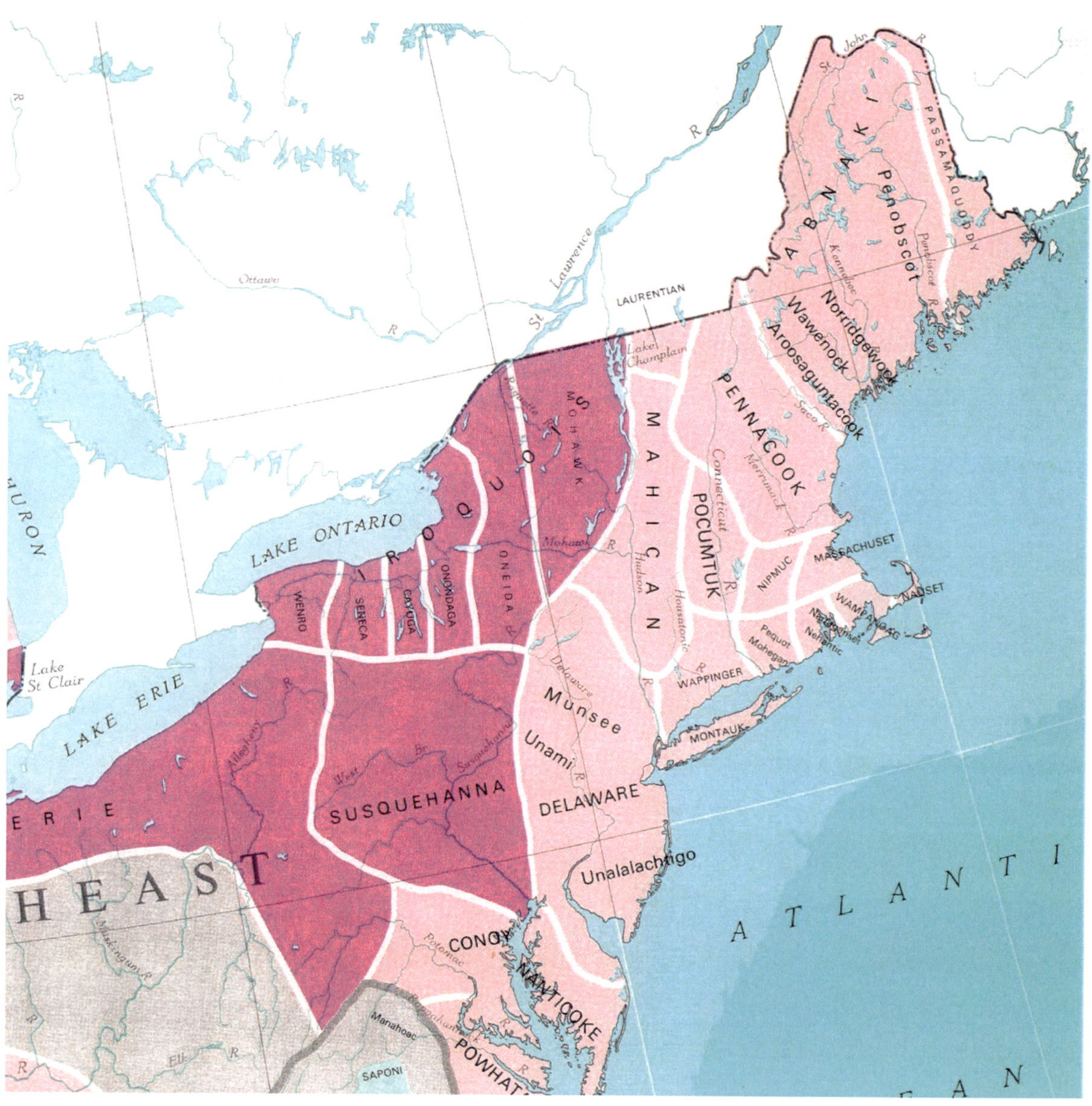

Map of "Early Indian Tribes, Culture Areas and Linguistic Stocks" made by William C. Sturtevant of the Smithsonian Institution in 1967. Public Domain. Most Native Americans living in the lighter shaded areas spoke Algonquian languages. Most of those in the darker shaded area spoke Iroquoian languages.

"The Indian Fort Sasquesehanok" near what is now York, Pennsylvania. Engraving by Jacob van Meurs (1671). Public Domain. The Susquehannock were an Iroquoian speaking nation who were often at war. Unlike the Lenni Lenape, most Iroquoians built palisades, or wooden walls around their villages. From the Journal of the Lancaster Historical Society, Volume 14, No. 3 (1910)

Another group of Algonquians settled in and around the Delaware River and Bay. One group on the west side of the Delaware River, by what are now Philadelphia and Delaware, called themselves Lenni Lenape, which means "original people." According to their legends, all of the Algonquian nations around them were once part of their tribe.

There were also small groups of Algonquians on the east side of the Delaware River in what is now New Jersey. They did not call themselves "Lenni Lenape."

They did not recognize or follow any Lenni Lenape "sachem" or chief. However, they "spoke the same language and lived in the same manner." They wandered throughout what are now New Jersey, eastern Pennsylvania, and southern New York. They had few permanent settlements in South Jersey.

European settlers and traders found this confusing. For convenience, they called all Native Americans in and around South Jersey "Lenni Lenape." They also called them the "Delaware". That is because they lived by the river and bay they named after Lord De La Warr. He was the Governor and Captain General of the English settlement in Jamestown, Virginia, in 1610.

In 1693, Gabriel Thomas described the Lenape-speaking natives of South Jersey as follows:

"They are very loving to one another. For if three or four of them come into a Christian's house, and the master of it happens to give one of them victuals, and none to the rest, he will divide it into equal shares among them. And they are also kind and civil to any of the Christians, for I have had victuals cut by them in their cabins before they took any for themselves.

"Their chief employment is hunting, fishing, and fowling, or making canoes or 'Indian boats' or 'bowls,' in all which arts they are dexterous and ingenious.

"Their women business chiefly outside in planting of Indian corn and pounding it to meal in mortars with pestils (as we beat our spice) and make bread, and dress their victuals, which they perform very neatly and cleanly. They also make Indian mats, ropes, hats and baskets (some of curious workmanship) with their hemp, which there grows wild and natural in the woods. . .

"Their houses are, for the most part, covered with chestnut bark, but very close and warm, insomuch that no rain can go through. . . Their habit is commonly deerskin or duffle (a coarse, heavy woolen material). . ."

Other Native Americans speaking an Iroquoian language also moved northeast. They included the Iroquois and Huron nations in what are now upstate New York, Quebec, and Ontario. They also included the Susquehannock by the Susquehanna River in what is now Pennsylvania. The Cherokee, also Iroquoians, later moved to what are now the Carolinas, Georgia, Alabama, and Tennessee.

Le Massacre des Hurons par les Iroquois (Massacre of Hurons by the Iroquois during 1649-1650), Joseph Legare (1827). Musée Beaux-arts du Québec by Wilfredor, First Nations by Wilfredor (2019). Wikimedia Commons.

Many Iroquois were aggressive. They often fought bitter and sometimes genocidal wars with nearby Algonquian nations and each other. The Iroquoian Susquehannock often attacked Lenni Lenape communities in what are now New Jersey and Eastern Pennsylvania.

However, some Algonquians, like the Powhatan in Virginia, were also aggressive. British scientist Thomas Harriott visited them and learned their language between 1584 and 1586. He described how they used ambushes and deception to attack and exterminate peaceful neighbors.

There were many aggressive and peaceful Native American nations, just as there were many aggressive and peaceful European nations. There were also warlike and peaceful factions within many Native American and European nations.

When Europeans arrived, peaceful or weaker Native American nations often helped and made alliances with Europeans to survive attacks by other Native Americans.

3.

Lenni Lenape speakers roam in and around what is now South Jersey.

There were only about 8,000 to 25,000 speakers of the Lenni Lenape language when the first Europeans arrived. They were spread out over an enormous area. They lived as far north as what is now Kingston, in upstate New York, and as far south as what is now Lewes, Delaware. They were as far east as what is now Long Island in New York, and as far west as the Pocono Mountains in what is now Pennsylvania.

Some lived in small groups of 50 to 100 people. Some lived in larger villages of several hundred.

For a time, groups of Iroquoian Susquehannock lived in and around what is now Burlington, New Jersey. During the 1600s, they fought wars with Lenni Lenape speaking nations.

The Iroquois and most nations around them usually built wooden walls, or palisades around their villages to protect them from attacks. So did the Powhatan

"The Swedes and the Indians in New Sweden." Engraving by Thomas Campanius Holm. Published in Kort Beskrifning om Provincien Nya Swerige uit America (Short Description of Province of New Sweden in America) in 1702. Source: Wikimedia Commons. Public Domain.

in Virginia. Lenni Lenape speakers rarely did so. They were known to move away from conflicts or settle disputes through negotiation and compromise when possible.

However, some Lenni Lenape speakers fought fiercely when provoked. One group fought a series of short but bitter wars against Dutch colonists near the Hudson River between 1643 and 1664.

"Two Lenni Lenape Men and a Child" drawn by Peter Lindestrom. Lindestrom was one of several hundred Swedes and Finns who settled in the "New Sweden" colony in and around Wilmington, New Castle, and Swedesboro between 1638 and 1664. He compiled his maps and drawings in a manuscript called "Geographia Americae" and placed them with the Royal Archives in Stockholm just before his death in 1691. They were later published by Thomas Campanius Holm in Sweden in 1702 and by Amandus Johnson for the Swedish Colonial Society in Philadelphia in 1925. Public Domain.

4.

Many Lenni Lenape near the Delaware River spend summers by the South Jersey shore.

Many Lenni Lenape from west of the Delaware River left their villages after planting their spring crops. They set up summer homes near the creeks, back bays, and beaches near the Atlantic Ocean and Delaware Bay. There they hunted, fished, and gathered clams and oysters. They called one back bay "Absegami," which means "Little Water." Today it is called Absecon Bay. The town of Absecon was later built along its mainland shore. The narrow island of sand on the other side of that bay was later called Absecon Island. Atlantic City is there today.

At the end of each summer, they returned to their villages across the Delaware River and Bay. There, they harvested their crops and stayed for the winter.

Lenape-speaking Native Americans catching and drying fish in the back bays by the shore of what is now New Jersey. Drawing by John T. Kraft. From The Lenape or Delaware Indians by Herbert C. Kraft. Published by Seton Hall University Museum in 1996. Image reproduced with permission of Seton Hall University Museum.

5.
A Turkish "Ghazi" in the Middle East starts events that bring Europeans to America.

In 1281, a Turkish "ghazi" captured much of a small province in the Byzantine, or Eastern Roman Empire, in the Middle East. A ghazi (also "gazi") was a Muslim raider who attacked and robbed towns and caravans of *kafirs* (nonbelievers) during *jihads* (religious wars). That set in motion a chain of events that brought Europeans to the Lenni Lenape in America.

That ghazi was known as "Osman" in Turkish and "Uthman" in Arabic. Most Europeans called him "Ottoman." The territory he took was in the ancient province of Bithynia. Most of its people had been Greek-speaking Christians since Saint Peter the Apostle preached there 1,200 years before.

Bithynia was near Constantinople, the largest city in Europe. Constantinople had been the capital of the Greek-speaking Eastern Roman Empire for a thousand years. It was one of the world's busiest and wealthiest commercial centers.

Later interpretation by an unknown artist of Sultan Gazi Uthman Han. He was also known as Osman I, the "Ghazi," and "Ottoman. Source: Wikimedia Commons. Public Domain.

Ships from the Mediterranean Sea passed by on their way to ports on the Black Sea. They carried goods from all over Europe, like wheat, honey, olive oil, leather, wine, knives, and swords. Caravans then took those goods to China. These goods were sold for silk, tea, and ceramics from China and spices from the Spice Islands (now Indonesia).

Italian merchants from Venice, Genoa, Florence, and Milan owned and sailed most of those ships. One of them, Marco Polo, wrote a famous book about his travels to China and the East.

The Ottomans, that is, Osman and his successors, ended that trade within a hundred years.

6.

Barbary and Turkish "Corsairs" make the Mediterranean dangerous for Italian merchants.

The Ottomans did what *ghazis* rarely did. They held and occupied the cities and towns they attacked. They quickly turned their small holdings in Bithynia into one of the most powerful empires in the world. They recruited, organized, and equipped large professional armies and navies. They ruled and taxed the people they conquered with ruthless efficiency.

By the 1400s, the Ottomans firmly controlled all of what is now Turkey, Greece, and most of Southeastern Europe. They also held most of the nearby islands and port cities that had been used by Italian merchants. In 1453, the Ottomans seized Constantinople itself. They renamed it Istanbul.

The Ottomans either subjugated or made alliances with Arab Muslims along the "Barbary Coast" of North Africa. That area included the port cities of Algiers, Tunis, and Tripoli.

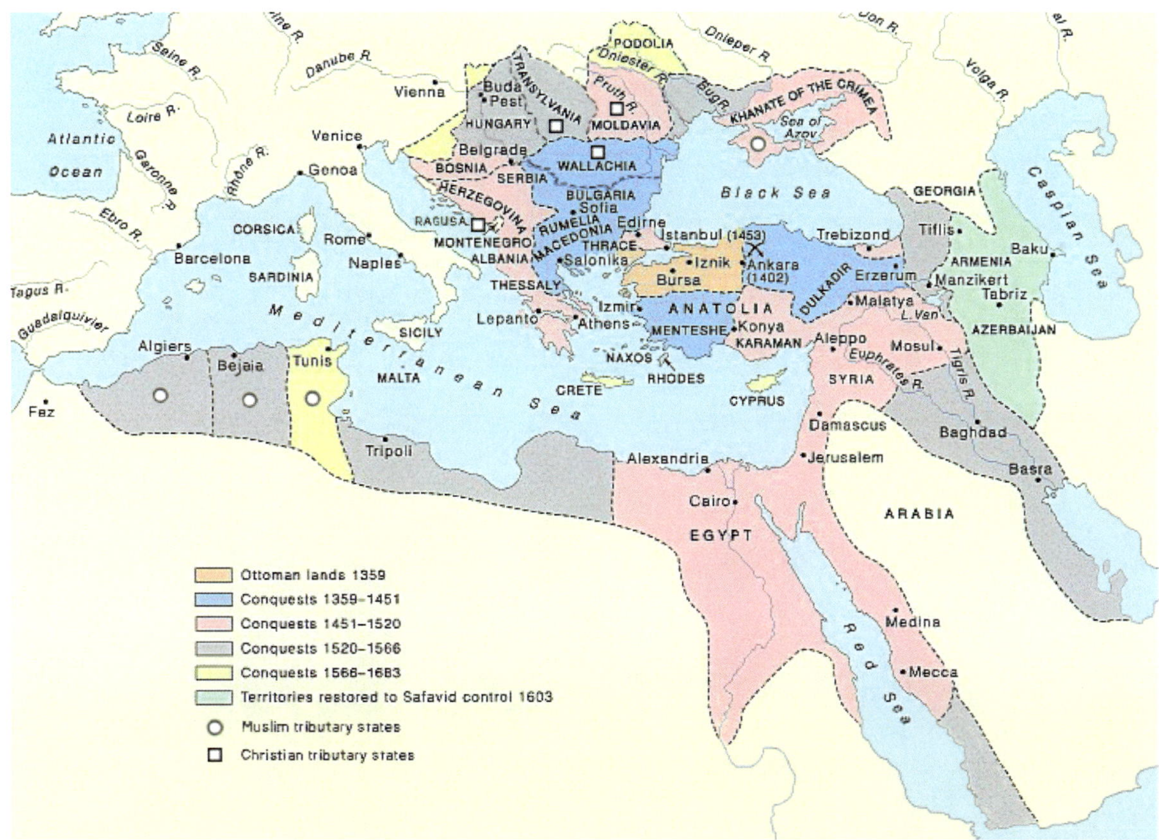

"Expansion of Ottoman Empire" (2009) RJJensen. https://www.conservapedia.com/File:Otexpand.jpg. Creative Commons Attribution-Share Alike. 3.0

The Ottomans and their allies in North Africa systematically attacked and robbed the ships and coastal towns of Italy and of all *kafir* (non-believer) nations unless they submitted and paid tribute.

Europeans often called them "Barbary pirates." However, pirates are criminals, and these raiders were not. They were instead "corsairs" or "privateers" with "letters of marque and reprisal". Those letters, given by the rulers of nations at war, were permits to legally attack and rob enemy ships and towns — as long as the "booty" was shared with the governments that issued them. The Ottomans and their Barbary allies were often at war with Christian nations in Europe and often used corsairs.

The most valuable booty was usually the crew of ships or the residents of coastal towns. They were either sold as slaves or held for ransom. Slaves with skills could stay alive for many years. Others were put to hard labor and died within months. Many were used as "galley slaves." They pulled the oars of Turkish and Barbary galleys until they died. Only a lucky few returned home.

This terrified European sailors. Most of the Mediterranean Sea became too dangerous and unprofitable for Italian merchants and their ships. Most fled to safer waters and harbors along the Atlantic Ocean.

A priest pays Ottoman Turks to free Christian slaves. Painting by Giovanni Maria Morandi (late 1600s). Source: Louvre Museum via Wikimedia Commons and Picryl. Public Domain.

7.

Italian sea captains cross the Atlantic. Columbus finds America and great wealth for Spain.

In 1317, a merchant sailor named Emanuele Pessagno left his home in Genoa, Italy. He moved to Portugal and changed his name to Manuel Pessanha. From there, he discovered new trade routes in the Atlantic Ocean along the coast of Africa. Later Portuguese explorers sailed farther south to the southern tip of Africa. There, they found a sea route to India and the East.

In 1495, Giovanni Caboto left Venice, Italy, and moved to England. There he went by the name of John Cabot. In 1497, King Henry VII of England sent Cabot, his son, and "two Venetians" across the Atlantic Ocean to look for a sea route to China. They landed in Newfoundland. They then sailed south along the coast to what is now Florida before returning. They claimed everything they saw for England. That included what is now New Jersey.

In 1506, Giovanni da Verrazano left Florence, Italy, and moved to France. In 1523, the King of France sent him across the Atlantic to look for a passage to the Pacific Ocean. Verrazano first sailed to what is now South Carolina. He then sailed

"The First Landing of Christopher Columbus": 1862 Painting by Dióscoro Teofilo de la Puebla Tolin on display in Museo del Prado, Madrid, Spain. Posted online by Wikimedia. Public Domain.

north along the coast until he reached Newfoundland. He explored many rivers and bays along the way. One of them was what we now call Raritan Bay by Sandy Hook and Staten Island. However, he did not find a passage to the Pacific Ocean.

In 1476, a sea captain named Christopher Columbus left Genoa, Italy. For the next ten years, he sailed ships in the Atlantic for Portugal. Then he sailed for Spain. In 1492, Columbus crossed the Atlantic, hoping to reach China. He found the Bahamas, Cuba, and other Caribbean islands instead. Later Spanish explorers found profitable sea routes to the East. They also found gold, silver and other riches in Mexico and South America. This made Spain the richest and most powerful nation in Europe.

Portrait of John Cabot (known in Italy as Giovanni Caboto) Painted by Giustino Menescardi (1762). From a mural in the Palazzo Ducal in Venice. Posted online by Wikimedia Commons. Public Domain.

8.

Spain fights costly wars against the Ottoman Turks and their Barbary allies.

After taking Constantinople in 1453, the Ottoman Turks went on to conquer more of Christian Europe. In 1521, they took the fortress cities of Belgrade and Szabacs in Serbia. In 1526, they occupied Hungary after destroying its army at Mohacs.

In 1529, the Turks tried but failed to take Vienna in the heart of Central Europe. Before they withdrew, they murdered and tortured thousands of Christians in farms and villages outside the city. They captured and took back thousands more as slaves. Vienna was part of the Holy Roman Empire ruled by Charles V, the King of Spain. Spain had sent soldiers to help defend the city.

Ottoman and Barbary corsairs also continued to attack and rob Spanish and Italian ships and towns in and around the Mediterranean Sea.

In 1560 Spain and several Italian states formed a "Holy League" to stop them. They sent warships and soldiers to North Africa. They hoped to "reconquer"

"Battle of Mohacs" Painting by Bertalan Szekely (1862). Hungarian National Gallery via Wikimedia Commons. Public Domain.

"The Battle of Lepanto." Painted by Laureys a Castro in 1683. Source: Wikimedia Commons from Bonhams .com Auctions. Public Domain.

those lands for Christendom just as Spain and Portugal were "reconquered" before. However, they failed.

In 1570, the Ottomans invaded the Christian island of Cyprus. Pope Pius V formed a new Holy League to defend it. Spain and several Italian states assembled a massive fleet with 212 warships and 28,500 soldiers. They arrived too late to save Cyprus. However, they destroyed the Ottoman fleet near its home port of Lepanto in Greece.

The Spanish and Italians again tried to seize the "Barbary" kingdoms of North Africa. However, they failed again.

By this time, Spain had spent much of its wealth from America and was heavily in debt. Spain did not build its own industries. It instead spent its gold and silver from America to buy goods from other countries. Spain also spent much of its money on constant wars. They included "Wars of Religion" against Protestant Christians as well as against Turkish and Barbary Muslims.

Portrait of Pope Pius V made by Bartolomeo Passarotti in 1566. Source: The Walters Art Museum via Wikimedia Commons. Public Domain.

9.

Spain also fights "wars of religion" against "Protestant" Christians. Its "Armada" fails to subdue England.

In 1519, King Charles V of Spain was elected Emperor of the Holy Roman Empire. That gave Spain power in Austria, Holland, Germany, and Italy. However, it also dragged Spain into long and costly "Wars of Religion" against Protestants in Europe.

Before then, almost all Christians in Europe were Catholics. The Pope ruled their churches from Rome. He appointed their priests and determined their worship and teachings. The Pope also selected, removed, and influenced many political leaders.

In 1410, Jan Hus, a Czech priest in Bohemia, publicly criticized several Catholic officials and practices. In 1415, he was arrested, condemned, and burned alive for heresy.

In 1517, Martin Luther, a German priest, posted "95 Theses" on the front door of his church in Wittenberg, Germany. They stated his core beliefs

Monument to Jan Hus in Prague, Czech Republic. Photo taken in 2019 and posted on Wikimedia Commons online by Yelkrokoyade under Creative Commons CC0 License.

and criticized the Pope and the Catholic Church. Luther claimed that every Christian could understand God's laws by reading the Bible. He said, "Every Christian a priest!" To make this possible, Luther translated the Bible into German. He then published it with newly invented printing presses. Luther also urged Christians to choose their own priests and run their own churches.

In 1521, Pope Leo X condemned Martin Luther as a heretic. In 1529, Charles V, as King of Spain and Holy Roman Emperor, declared war on Luther and his followers. Luther and his supporters "protested" this and fought back. They became known as "Protestants." Their struggle against the Pope and Catholic Church became known as the "Protestant Reformation."

In 1534, King Henry VIII of England also opposed the Pope. He took all the churches in England out of the Pope's control and formed a new "Church of England." However, the English King was no Protestant. He did it only so he could divorce his Spanish wife and marry a woman who could give him a male heir. Henry VIII avoided war with Spain. He brutally persecuted and executed followers of Martin Luther, who translated the Bible and taught it in English.

Henry VIII died in 1547. His only son, Edward VI, was only nine years old. He died six years later. Henry's oldest daughter Mary was then made Queen. She was a militant Catholic who viciously persecuted Protestants. She became known as "Bloody Mary" when she executed 283 Protestant leaders, mostly by burning them alive. Mary died without children in 1558.

Elizabeth, the youngest legitimate child of Henry VIII, was then made Queen. Elizabeth was a Protestant who appointed Protestants to run the Church of England. This angered the Catholic kings of Spain. In 1588, Spain sent an "Armada" to invade England and restore Catholic control. That Armada was a massive force of 137 ships, 10,000 sailors, 52,000 soldiers, and 2,500 cannons. It was defeated and destroyed by severe Atlantic storms, unknown rocks and shoals, and a smaller, but more mobile, English navy.

"English Fireships Attacking Spanish Armada in 1588". Painting by an unknown Flemish artist in 1590. On display in the National Maritime Museum, Greenwich, England. Source: Wikimedia Commons. Public Domain.

10.

England fails to reach China when it sails North and West. Its settlers starve in Jamestown.

Spain and Portugal both reached China and the Spice Islands of the East by sailing south in the Atlantic Ocean. Spain sailed below South America and then west. Portugal sailed south below Africa, and then east.

England tried to reach China and the East by sailing north. In 1553, it sent Hugh Willoughby to explore the Arctic Ocean north of Russia. He was trapped by ice and froze to death. In 1607, Henry Hudson tried to sail over the North Pole but was blocked by ice. He mistakenly thought that the ice there melted during the long days of summer. In 1609, Hudson looked for a "northwest passage" to China above Canada. He got as far as Hudson Bay as winter approached. When Hudson refused to turn back, his crew mutinied. They put him and his son on a small boat and left them to die.

England also hoped to find gold and silver in North America. In 1587, Sir Walter Raleigh "planted" 115 settlers near the Outer Banks of what is now North Carolina. He called it Roanoke. However, that colony was "lost."

"Death of Sir Hugh Willoughby in 1554."
By unknown artist. Source: Wikimedia
Commons. Public Domain.

"The Last Voyage of Henry Hudson
(1609)." Painted by John Collier in 1881.
Source Tate Britain Art Museum via
Wikimedia Commons. Public Domain.

Because of the Spanish Armada, a ship with fresh supplies could not return to Roanoke until three years later. When it arrived, it found no trace of the settlers. Some may have intermarried with Native Americans. However, there is much evidence that they were attacked and massacred by Powhatan, the father of Pocahontas.

Between 1607 and 1609, English investors formed a new company to "plant" a settlement or "plantation" in "Virginia". At that time, the name "Virginia" was used by the English to describe all of North America between Newfoundland and Florida. This was to honor their "Virgin Queen" Elizabeth, who never married.

When Elizabeth died in 1603, James became the first King to rule over both England and Scotland as the "United Kingdom". The new settlement in Virginia was named "Jamestown" after him.

"Burial of the Dead 1609-1610." Painting by Sidney E. King (1950) for the National Park Service. Courtesy of Encyclopedia Virginia, Charlottesville, VA. Creative Commons Attribution-NonCommercial-ShareAlike License.

The first settlers of Jamestown spent much of their time searching for gold. However, they failed to clear enough land and grow enough crops. Most died from hunger during the winter of 1609-1610. That winter became known as "The Starving Time."

11.

Land, liberty, and slaves save Jamestown.

After the "Starving Time," the Virginia Company changed how it ran Jamestown. Until then, all land was owned by the Company. Everyone who worked on that land was either a company employee or an indentured servant.

Employees were paid wages. Indentured servants had sold their freedom for a fixed number of years to pay their debts and for passage to America. During that time, they received no pay other than food, clothing, and shelter.

All harvests were put in the company storehouse. Surpluses were kept by the Company as its profit. Company officials made most decisions on running the colony from London, 4,000 miles away.

In 1613, the Company changed that. It gave each family a 3-acre plot of land and enough time off to work it. The Company increased that to 50 acres per family in 1616 and 100 acres in 1618.

In 1619, the Company changed its charter to let these new landowners elect a 22-member *House of Burgesses*. "Burgess," like "freeholder," was an old English

"Jamestown Lifescape," depicting life in the settlement around 1650. Painted by Keith Rocco, Artist for the National Park Service in 1997. On Display at Colonial National Historical Park, Virginia. National Parks Gallery. Public Domain.

word for landowner. These elected representatives of landowners now made most decisions for the colony.

Harvests increased immediately. Men, women, and children worked long hours to clear their own land and to plant, weed, fertilize, and harvest their own crops.

Another important event happened in 1619. Dutch privateers in the Caribbean Sea captured a Portuguese ship taking 350 African slaves from Angola to Spanish sugar plantations in Mexico.

The Dutch took 20 of the slaves to Jamestown and traded them for food and supplies.

At that time, there was no slavery in England or Jamestown. There were no laws permitting people to be bought, sold, or owned as slaves. The Africans were sold with the same indentured servant contracts used for whites. They and their children were set free at the end of their years of service. Some later purchased other Africans as their slaves.

However, Jamestown soon changed those laws. By 1641, Jamestown had adopted many laws that the British colony of Barbados had adopted to permit

Tobacco Farming in Jamestown, 1619. Painting made by J. Paul Hudson for the National Park Service in 1956, based on research. Source. Wikimedia Commons. Public Domain.

the permanent enslavement of Africans there. Africans in Virginia were then bought, sold, and owned as slaves and not as indentured servants. They, their children, and their grandchildren never became free unless their owners chose to free them. South Carolina and other English colonies in North America soon adopted similar laws.

With land, liberty, and slaves, the Jamestown settlers soon produced far more food than they needed. They also grew tobacco and other cash crops. Their colony became prosperous and expanded.

In 1622, Powhatan warriors from nearby villages launched a surprise attack on Jamestown. They killed 347 settlers. That was roughly one fourth of the population. However, the remaining settlers survived and fought back. They defeated the Powhatan the following year. Many new settlements were then "planted" nearby. They included "plantations" further up the James River, on the York River, and along the Chesapeake Bay. Virginia prospered and grew.

"Landing Negroes at Jamestown from Dutch man-of-war, 1619." Harpers Magazine (1901). Source: Library of Congress via Wikimedia Commons. Public Domain.

12.

Slavery is normal in most of the world.

When the first black Africans were brought to Jamestown, slavery was normal in most of the world. India and China had slaves. Native Americans attacked, captured, and enslaved people from weaker nations long before Europeans arrived.

Slavery was common in Africa. The Kongo and Mbundu were large, warlike nations that lived in what are now Angola and the Democratic Republic of the Congo. The Imbangala were an aggressive, militarized cult that roamed throughout the area. Warriors from all three groups attacked and enslaved members of weaker tribes. During the 1500s, Portuguese merchant ships often stopped along the coast of Angola on their way to and from India. The Kongo, Mbundu, and Imbangala traded many of their slaves to the Portuguese in exchange for guns, ammunition, and other European goods.

Slavery was also an important part of the Islamic world. Islamic law or "sharia" permitted Muslims to make slaves of non-believers they captured during war.

"Arab Slave Trading Caravan" (c. 1860). Probably from Drawing by John Frederick Lewis. Wikimedia Commons. Public Domain.

In 627, Muhammad enslaved non-believers when he conquered Medina in Arabia. During the next hundred years, his followers enslaved large numbers of Christians, Persians, and Hindus in the vast areas they conquered from the Atlantic Ocean to India.

For the next thousand years, Arabs and Berbers from the "Barbary" kingdoms of North Africa sent warships to capture European Christians and bring them back as slaves. After the 1300s, they were joined by the Ottoman Turks. Between 1530 and 1780, they captured and sold more than a million European Christians as slaves from ships and coastal villages as far away as Iceland.

During this time, they also sent raiding parties south across the Sahara Desert. Arabs in Egypt and the Middle East sailed down the Nile River and the Indian

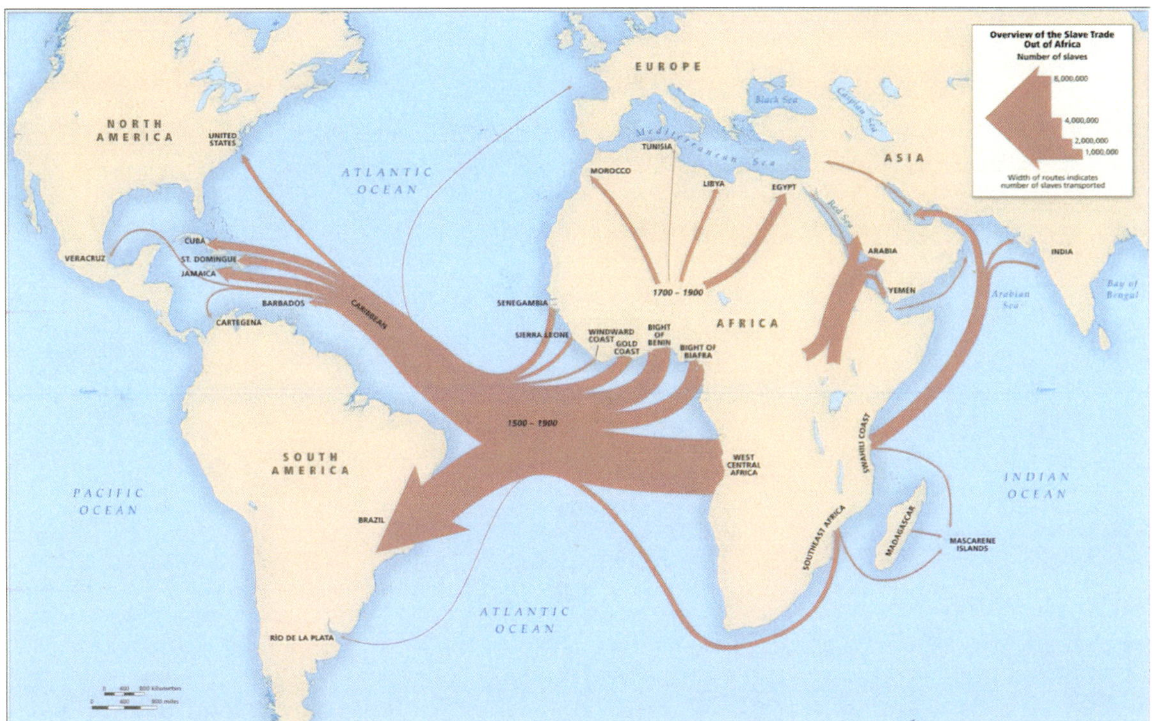

"Overview of the Transatlantic Slave Trade, 1500-1900." From Atlas of the Transatlantic Slave Trade (2010, a copyrighted work of Yale University Press. (This chart is misleading in that it shows the number of black Africans brought across the Atlantic Ocean for a 350-year period from 1500 until the end of that slave trade in 1850. However, it shows enslaved Blacks brought across the Sahara Desert to Islamic countries for only a 200-year period from 1700 to 1900.) Used with permission from Yale University Press.

Ocean. They brought back so many black Africans as slaves that "abd/abeed," the Arabic words for "slave/slaves," also mean black African/Africans to many speakers of Arabic today. Roughly 3.5 to 10 million black Africans were sold as slaves in the Islamic world between the years 650 and 1600 AD. Few descendants of those slaves are alive today. Most of the men were castrated soon after being captured.

Slavery ended in most of Christian Europe by the 1200s. However, it continued in Spain and Portugal, where Christians and Muslims often enslaved each other during the many wars of the "Reconquista" (Reconquest). During the 1500s, Portugal began using black African slaves they bought in Angola to grow and process sugarcane in Brazil. The Portuguese made such enormous profits that the Spanish, Dutch, English, and French then set up their own colonies in the Caribbean to do the same. They also bought and transported black slaves from Africa to work there.

During the 1500s, Europeans brought roughly 328,000 black Africans as slaves to Brazil and the Caribbean. During those same hundred years, Arabs captured or bought roughly 750,000 black Africans for sale as slaves in the Islamic world.

Europeans then greatly increased their use of slaves from Africa. They brought 1,348,000 across the Atlantic during the 1600s, 6,090,000 during the 1700s, and 3,466,000 during the 1800s. More than half of them were taken to Brazil.

Britain and the United States outlawed the transportation of slaves from Africa in 1807 and 1808. Spain and France did the same in 1815 and 1820. Brazil became the last nation to stop bringing African slaves to America in 1850.

Europeans brought a total of roughly 11 million black Africans across the Atlantic as slaves during those 350 years between 1500 and 1850.

About 460,000, or 4% of black Africans taken across the Atlantic, were taken to the British colonies of North America that later became the United States. Roughly 390,000 were brought directly from Africa. Another 60,000 to 70,000 were brought indirectly through the Caribbean.

During those same 350 years, Arabs (including North African Berbers) brought more than five million black Africans to the Islamic world as slaves. The number increased from roughly 750,000 during the 1500s, to roughly 900,000 in the 1600s, 1,300,000 in the 1700s, and 2,150,000 in the 1800s. During the mid-1800s, England and France took action to end slavery in Africa. They were later joined by other European colonial powers. Most slaves in Africa were freed by the early 1900s.

13.

England lets "Separatists"
run their own churches
if they go to North America.

In 1534, King Henry VIII and Parliament took all churches in England away from the Pope. They then ruled them through their new Church of England.

However, neither the King nor Parliament were Protestants. They broke away from the Pope's "Catholic" Church only so King Henry VIII could divorce his wife and marry a woman who could give him a male heir.

Between 1509 and 1547, King Henry VIII arrested and executed at least 63 ministers, scholars, and others who promoted the Protestant doctrines of Martin Luther or who in any way criticized the Church of England.

Most were tied to a stake and burned alive for "heresy." They included Dr. Robert Barnes and two Lutheran ministers who were executed in 1540.

Roughly 200 other Protestants were executed after King Henry VIII by King Edward VI, Queen Mary, Queen Elizabeth, and King James I. Many more had their lands and other property seized.

During the early 1600s, worshippers in a remote country village called Scrooby refused to let the King's "rector" (parish priest) run their church. They chose their own ministers and developed their own teachings. They often held worship services in their homes.

They were called "Separatists," Some were dismissed from government positions. Others were threatened with arrest or loss of property. In 1609, many of them fled to the city of Leiden in Holland. However, they did not want to settle there. They did not want their children to lose their English language and culture.

In 1620, the King and Parliament chartered another "Virginia Company" to "plant"

(Dr. Robert) Barnes and his Fellow Prisoners Seeking Forgiveness." Illustration from Foxe's Book of Martyrs, published by Joseph Martin Kronheim in 1887. Posted online by Wikimedia Commons. Public Domain.

a settlement or "plantation" in North America. To attract settlers, they offered religious freedom there as well as land and self-government. The "Separatists" of Leiden returned to England when they got permission to settle in North America. They left on the ship *Mayflower* in 1620. Their settlement later became known as the "Plymouth Plantation."

14.

The Pilgrims starve when " the community" owns all land. They feast and give thanks when each family farms its own parcel.

Storms took the Mayflower to land that was far north of Jamestown. However, after exploring the area, its passengers agreed to settle there. They named the area "Plymouth." Since their contract with the Virginia Company no longer applied, they made a written agreement to run the settlement themselves. It became known as *The Mayflower Compact*. Those settlers are now known as The Pilgrims.

The Pilgrims found many fields nearby that were already cleared and ready for planting. A Native American named Squanto later approached them. He explained that those fields had belonged to members of his tribe. He said they all had died from a plague a few years before. Squanto befriended the Pilgrims and taught them how to grow native crops like corn, beans, and squash.

However, the Pilgrims failed to grow enough food. Many died of hunger during the first two years. As in Jamestown, there was no private ownership of land.

"The First Thanksgiving" (1912). Painting by Jean Leon Gerome Ferris. Public Domain.

All harvested crops were put into a common storehouse and distributed according to the needs of each family.

During the third year, the Pilgrims divided the land and gave each family its own plot. As in Jamestown, everyone worked much longer and harder for themselves and their families than they did for the community. The Pilgrims then had "bounteous" harvests and gave thanks. They quickly became prosperous and self-sufficient.

William Bradford, their Governor, explained this in his journal.

"No supply (ship) was heard of, neither knew they when they might expecte any. So they begane to thinke how they might raise as much corne as they could, and obtaine a beter crope then they had done, that they might not still thus languish in miserie. At length, after much debate of things, the Governor (with the advise

of the cheefest amongest them) gave way that they should set corne every man for his owne perticuler, and in that regard trust to them selves; in all other things to goe on in the generall way as before. And so assigned to every family a parcell of land, according to the proportion of their number for that end, only for present use (but made no devission for inheritance), and ranged all boys & youth under some familie.

"This had very good success; for it made all hands very industrious, so as much more corne was planted then other wise would have bene by any means the Governor or any other could use, and saved him a great deall of trouble, and gave farr better contente. The women now wente willingly into the feild, and tooke their litle-ons with them to set corne, which before would aledg weaknes, and inabilitie; whom to have compelled would have bene thought great tiranie and oppression.

Bradford then reflected on this "experience." He wrote that it exposed the "vanity" and "conceit" of "godly and sober men" and "ancient" philosophers who advocated community control and ownership of what Communists today call the "means of production."

"(They claimed) that the taking away of propertie, and bringing in comunitie into a comone wealth, would make them happy and florishing; as if they were wiser then God.

"For this comunitie (so farr as it was) was found to breed much confusion & discontent, and retard much imployment that would have been to their benefite and comforte. For the yong-men that were most able and fitte for labour & service did repine (express discontent) that they should spend their time & streingth to worke for other mens wives and children, with out any recompence. The strong, or man of parts, had no more in devission of victails & cloaths, then he that was weake and not able to doe a quarter the other could; this was thought injustice. The aged and graver men to be ranked and equalised in labours, and victails, cloaths, &c., with the meaner & yonger sorte, thought it some indignite & disrespect unto them. And for mens wives to be commanded to doe servise for other men, as dresing their meate, washing their cloaths, &c., they deemd it a kind

of slaverie, neither could many husbands well brooke it. Upon the poynte all being to have alike, and all to doe alike, they thought them selves in the like condition, and one as good as another; and so, if it did not cut of those relations that God hath set amongest men, yet it did at least much diminish and take of the mutuall respects that should be preserved amongst them. And would have bene worse if they had been men of another condition. Let none objecte this is men›s corruption, and nothing to the course it selfe. I answer, seeing all men have this corruption in them, God in his wisdome saw another course fiter for them. . . "

This "experience" of the Pilgrims dominated the culture, economy, and politics of America for the next 350 years.

Soon afterwards, English "Puritans" obtained a charter from King Charles to establish a new "Massachusetts Bay Colony" north of Plymouth. They quickly established Salem, Boston and other large settlements and towns there.

Those Puritans were much like the "separatist" Pilgrims of Plymouth. They had similar beliefs and worshipped in the same way.

However, the Puritans wanted to control and "purify" the Church of England rather than separate from it. While in America, they wanted their colonial government to impose their "correct" Protestant beliefs on everyone living there. Besides Catholics, they also persecuted Quakers, Baptists, Anglicans and other Protestants who openly disagreed with them.

In 1632, King Charles established the colony of Maryland as a place in America where Catholics could freely practice their faith. In 1789, after American independence, Pope Pius VI allowed Catholics living in America to choose their own bishop. They chose John Carroll, a priest from Baltimore.

In 1636, two groups of Protestant "dissenters" bought land outside the Massachusetts Bay Colony and moved there. They later established the separate colonies of Connecticut and Rhode Island. Rhode Island was the first British colony in America to formally recognize and protect religious freedom for all.

15.

The Dutch conquer and settle by the Delaware River when England is weak from civil wars.

During the 1500s, Protestant England and the Netherlands (Holland) were often allies in wars of religion against Catholic Spain and Portugal. However, in 1652, those two Protestant countries fought the first of four wars against each other over colonies and trade.

When its wars against Holland began, England was weak and divided. Its troubles had begun in 1642. That was when England's King Charles I tried to rule without Parliament as an absolute monarch. He raised tariffs and various user fees on his own when Parliament refused to approve taxes he requested. The King also took military action without the consent of Parliament. Then the King tried to arrest members of Parliament who opposed him.

Parliament, led by Oliver Cromwell, formed its own army and fought back. It recruited a motley collection of veteran soldiers and untrained citizens.

In 1645, after several defeats, Parliament formed a "New Model Army." It appointed and promoted officers based on talent and achievement rather than wealth and privilege. To reduce class and regional differences, and confusion on the battlefield, all soldiers in the infantry were issued uniforms of a single color—"Venetian red". This is when British soldiers first became known as "redcoats." They defeated the King's army led by aristocrats, who were often called "cavaliers."

The "English Civil Wars" were also fought over religion. Cromwell and most of his supporters in Parliament were "Puritans." They wanted to "purify" the Church of England by "cleansing" it of all prayers, processions, rituals, decorations, and religious objects not based on the Bible. They wanted a clergy that did not dress or act like royalty.

"Oliver Cromwell at the Battle of Marton Moore, 1644" Unknown artist. Sometimes attributed to Abraham Cooper (1819) or Ernest Crofts (1877). Public Domain. Source: Wikimedia Commons.

They specifically opposed William Laud, the Archbishop of Canterbury appointed by King Charles I. The King was married to a Catholic, and Laud ran the Church of England much as the Pope ran the Roman Catholic Church. In 1641, Parliament arrested and imprisoned the Archbishop. In 1644, it put him on trial. However, there was not enough evidence to convict him of any crime. In 1645, Parliament enacted a "bill of attainder" that simply declared the Archbishop to be a traitor. He was then beheaded.

Trial of Archbishop Laud in 1644. Drawn by Alexander Johnston around 1890. Published in The Church of England: A History for the People by Henry Donald Maurice Spence-Jones (1898). Public Domain. Source: Wikimedia Commons.

In 1649, Parliament captured King Charles I and executed him for treason. The King's sons, Charles II and James, escaped to France and fought from exile.

After Parliament executed both the King and the Archbishop of Canterbury, the Puritans had absolute control of the Church of England. They persecuted all Protestant "Separatists" who believed that each congregation should control its own church. They also persecuted Catholics and "high church" Protestants who tried to continue Catholic worship traditions.

While the British were divided and weak, the Dutch were united, rich, and strong. The Dutch built many new ships and increased their trade and profits. They established and expanded new colonies and trading posts around the world.

"View of New Amsterdam" (1664) by Johannes Vingboons. Library of Congress through Picryl.com. Public Domain.

In 1623, the Dutch built "Fort Nassau" (now Gloucester City, New Jersey) by the Delaware River. In 1624, they built "Fort Orange" (now Albany in upstate New York) where the Mohawk River met the Hudson. In 1626, they built "New Amsterdam" on Manhattan Island. In 1630, they built Bergen (now "Old Bergen" in Jersey City).

The Dutch also settled elsewhere along the Hudson River and on Long Island. In 1655, they seized the Swedish and Finnish settlements along the Delaware River. The Dutch called their settlements in North America "New Netherland."

"Map of New Netherland, New England and Parts of Virginia" (1650) By Nicolaes Visscher. (Reprinted with new captions in 1685). Source: Library of Congress through Wikimedia Commons. Public Domain.

16.

Parliament unites England. King Charles II and James drive out the Dutch and create New Jersey.

Oliver Cromwell died in 1658 at the age of 59. In 1660, a newly elected Parliament invited both sons of Charles I back from exile. It installed his oldest son, Charles II, as King, and his younger son, James, Duke of York, as "Lord Admiral" of the Royal Navy. One of their top priorities was to put the Dutch back in their place.

They immediately adopted a new "Navigation Act." It made a list of products that merchants and producers in British colonies could only sell to Britain. They also had to use only British-owned ships to deliver them. They could no longer trade with Dutch merchants, who often offered better deals. They could no longer use Dutch ports.

Charles II and James then plotted to seize New Netherland. Dutch merchants there had direct access to the profitable Great Lakes trade in beaver skins through the Hudson and Mohawk rivers. They had convenient and strategic harbors near the Hudson and Delaware Rivers.

Trade with Dutch merchants in New Netherland also allowed Puritans and Separatists in New England to become too strong and independent. The new royals wanted new obedient British colonies next to them. Those new colonies were to be run by trusted supporters of the King—men like George Carteret and John Berkeley.

Both Carteret and Berkeley had commanded forces loyal to the King during the English Civil Wars. Both now secretly made plans with Charles and James to seize New Netherland from the Dutch. In January of 1664, they believed they could do it quickly without a war.

On February 10, 1664, Berkeley and Carteret secretly signed

Painting of James, Duke of York by Peter Lely around 1670. Royal Collection Trust. Public Domain.

"The Concession and Agreement" for the "Province of New Jersey." It was a constitution for a new British colony that would replace the Dutch colony of New Netherland. This was territory legally owned and occupied by the Dutch under a 1654 peace treaty made with England's previous government.

James, Berkeley and Carteret named their new colony after the Isle of Jersey in the English Channel. During the English Civil Wars, it became famous as a fortress and sanctuary for supporters of the King.

The Dutch Surrender New Amsterdam to England, September 8, 1664. Lithograph by Henry Alexander Ogden, Printed in 1897 in Ellis' History of Our Country. Public Domain.

One month later, King Charles secretly gave his brother James a deed to all of "New England." It ran from "New Scotland" (Nova Scotia) in the north to "Delaware Bay" in the south. This made James the owner of most of New Netherland. It also gave him direct control of the existing British colonies of Massachusetts Bay, Plymouth, Connecticut and Rhode Island.

James and Parliament then secretly appointed Captain Richard Nicolls to command an invasion force. They also made him Governor of the territory he was to conquer. Nicolls left England with four warships and 300 to 400 soldiers on May 25, 1664.

While Nicolls was at sea, James secretly signed a deed giving ownership and control of New Jersey to George Carteret and John Berkeley.

During this time, the British repeatedly told Dutch officials that they had no intention of breaking their 1654 peace treaty with Holland or seizing any of their territories.

Nicolls and his fleet reached Manhattan at the end of August. By the end of September of 1664, the British had captured all of New Netherland, from Long Island to Delaware Bay, without a fight. Nicolls renamed it "New York" after James, Duke of York.

In February of 1665, Berkeley and Carteret publicly claimed their ownership of New Jersey. They then published the "Concessions" that they had secretly signed the year before.

The Concessions were written to attract settlers to New Jersey and make its land valuable. They guaranteed everyone who settled there the same "freedoms and immunities" they had in England. They also gave settlers a new right to "freely and fully have and enjoy… their judgments and consciences in matters of religion."

"Philip Carteret Meets Settlers at Achter Coll (Now Elizabeth) in 1665" Mural by Howard Pyle at Essex County Courthouse painted in 1906. Public Domain.

The Concessions also offered free land to the first settlers. Men who came in the first year with "a good musket, bullets, powder", and "six months provision" were to get 150 acres. Others would get 30 to 100 acres.

Finally, the Concessions offered self-government. Everyone who owned land was a "freeholder." All freeholders could vote and hold public office. An "Assembly" elected by freeholders would make "laws, acts, and constitutions" and "lay equal taxes and assessments" for the colony.

The Concessions attracted much attention and praise when they were published. Berkeley and Carteret believed they would quickly survey and sell their land in New Jersey for a large profit. They appointed Philip Carteret, a relative of George Carteret, as their first Governor. They sent him and James Carteret, one of George Carteret's sons, to the newly built town of "Elizabethtown" (now Elizabeth). Both immediately got an unpleasant surprise.

Captain Richard Nicolls had been the Governor of New York since he had driven out the Dutch. Nicolls had already surveyed, divided, and sold half a million acres of the best land in New Jersey!

Nicolls assumed he was the Governor of all of what had been New Netherland. He did not know that James had created a new and separate colony of New Jersey across the Hudson River. He did not know that Berkeley and Carteret now owned it.

When James was told of this, he quickly voided all New Jersey land sales made by Nicolls. However, the buyers refused to leave the land they paid for. They also refused to pay a second time. Some threatened violence and rebellion.

The Carterets eventually honored most of the land sales made by Nicolls. However, they then tried to collect yearly fees or "quit-rents" for those properties.

"Cornelis Evertsen the Younger" (1680), Painting by Nicolaes Maes. Source: Rijksmuseum SK-A-1662. Public Domain.

In 1672, rioters forced Governor Philip Carteret and his family out of their home. Then George Carteret ordered his son James to move to land he owned in another new British colony called Carolina.

One year later, the Dutch gave Berkeley and Carteret another unpleasant surprise. The Dutch were at war with England for the third time since 1652. This time, the Dutch surprised the British. In 1673, a Dutch fleet commanded by Cornelis Evertsen the Younger sailed up the Hudson River. He captured New York without a fight and held it for a year. The Dutch gave New York back to Britain only after the British exchanged it for a more profitable colony in South America.

Lord John Berkeley was now 71 years old and heavily in debt. After nine years, he had gained nothing from New Jersey. He was eager to sell his half for whatever he could get.

"George Fox, The First Quaker." 1914 Facsimile of Portrait in Stone Made by Thomas Fairland (1804-1852) Source: Library of Congress. Public Domain.

17.

George Fox starts the "Quaker" movement in England. Thousands of his followers are persecuted and arrested.

George Fox was a charismatic and revolutionary Christian leader in England. He attracted a large following during its civil wars. Fox began preaching in 1647 when he was 23 years old. He began as a Protestant "Dissenter." He agreed with Martin Luther that every Christian can learn God's truths by reading the Bible. He did not believe that Christians needed a professional, ordained clergy to instruct them.

However, Fox went further. He taught that besides the Bible, each of the "faithful" also has an "inner light" to "illuminate man's sinfulness and lead in the way of truth and righteousness."

Fox and his followers called themselves "Children of the Light," "Friends of the Truth," the "Religious Society of Friends," or simply "Friends." At first, only their detractors called them "Quakers."

Quakers rejected the leadership, rituals, and formalities of all churches, not just the Church of England. They refused to pay "tithes." Tithes were a ten per-cent tax on each family's income to support the "established" (government--funded) Church of England.

Quakers refused to swear oaths. They did not swear allegiance to the King. They did not swear when testifying in court. They opposed war. They refused to take up arms for either side during the English Civil Wars.

Quakers gave leadership roles to women. Many opposed slavery and the slave trade. Quakers, including women, openly preached and distributed their literature in the streets. They aggressively sought converts. Some even disrupted services at other churches.

Many Quakers addressed others with the archaic singular pronouns "thou" and "thee" instead of the plural "you." In most of Europe, royalty at court was addressed with the plural "you." Later, it was "courteous" to address everyone that way. Many non-Quakers were offended by Quakers who addressed them with "thou" or "thee" instead.

Quakers taught both boys and girls to read. They taught the importance of being disciplined, thrifty, hard-working, and self-sufficient.

Quakers expected "Friends" to "keep to a word" and "not to trade beyond their abilities" in business. They were to settle disputes through negotiation and arbitration. They were to avoid lawsuits in courts run by non-Quakers whenever possible.

Young women were cautioned to wear "modest apparel" and avoid "broidered hair or gold or pearls or costly array."

Those who failed to meet these standards were "disowned." That meant they were excluded from worship services and meetings.

"George Fox Preaching in a Tavern in England in 1650" Watercolor by Edward Henry Wehnert (1865), Public Domain.

Quakers organized themselves into local and regional groups called "meetings." Each local group met each month to discuss issues, solve problems, and conduct business. It also sent representatives to semi-yearly or yearly meetings of all groups in the region.

Quakers built networks of "Friends" to help each other throughout Great Britain and its colonies.

All of this helped Quakers achieve spectacular success in almost every business, trade, and profession.

However, this also caused much envy, dislike, and mistrust of Quakers. Quakers were often harassed, attacked, and physically beaten in the streets. Many were dismissed from government positions, stripped of their property, and jailed.

By 1660, there were roughly 50,000 Quakers in England. In 1685, roughly 1,300 of them were in English prisons. George Fox was jailed eight times. Many Quakers fled to Massachusetts, Jamaica, Barbados, and other English colonies in America. Others fled to Holland or Dutch settlements in New Netherland. However, many were also persecuted there.

18.

Jurors find William Penn "not guilty" and are sent to jail.

William Penn was born in England in 1644. His father was an officer in the Royal Navy. Penn's father later became an influential and respected admiral who loaned money to Charles II and helped him become King.

In 1661, when William Penn was 17 years old, King Charles II issued a Proclamation making it "unlawful" for Quakers to meet without government permission. It also stated that Quakers were "avowed enemies of our lawful authority" who committed "insurrections and murders."

Five years later, William Penn rejected his father's Church of England and became a Quaker. Penn claimed that the King's Proclamation was ridiculous. He said it was obvious that Quakers were harmless, unarmed pacifists.

Penn tried to work around the King's Proclamation of 1661. Instead of having meetings, he and other Quakers spoke and worshipped at open outdoor gatherings.

In 1670, 26-year-old William Penn was arrested and indicted for "preaching" and "speaking" to roughly 300 people on a busy London street.

William Penn Appealing to the Jury During his 1670 Trial. Source: Bryant, William Cullen and Sydney Howard Gay. A Popular History of the United States. New York: Charles Scribners' Sons, 1881. From USHistoryImages.com. Public Domain.

Penn's defense was that Quakers had an "indispensable duty. . . to meet, preach, pray and praise God."

When the Judge asked Penn for his plea, Penn replied,

"I affirm I have broken no law. . . I desire that you let me know by what law it is you prosecute me."

The Judge responded, "Upon the common law."

Penn said, "If the law be common, it should not be so hard to produce it!"

When the Judge asked, "Are you guilty of this indictment?", Penn answered,

"The Question is not whether I am guilty of this indictment, but whether the indictment is legal. It is too general and imperfect to say it is the Common Law, unless we knew both where and what it is. For where there is no law, there is no transgression. And that law which is not in being is so far from being Common that it is no law at all!"

When the Judge ordered Penn to be taken back to the "bail-dock," Penn spoke to the jury:

"I speak for the fundamental laws of England. . . If these ancient fundamental laws which relate to Liberty and Property (only protect some "particular" religious groups) "who can say he hath the right to the coat upon his back!"

"Certainly, our liberties are open to be invaded, our wives be ravished, our children slaved, our families ruined, and our estates led away in triumph by every sturdy beggar and malicious informer as their trophies!"

The Judge then instructed the Jury: "You heard what the indictment is. It is preaching to the people and drawing a tumultuous company after them, and Mr. Penn was speaking. There are three or four witnesses that proved this. . ."

After deliberating for a "considerable time," the jurors found Penn "Guilty of Speaking in Gracechurch Street." They refused to find him guilty of any crime.

The judge then ordered the jury to be locked up without "meat, drink, fire and tobacco" until they delivered "a verdict the court will accept."

Two days later, the jury returned a verdict of "Not Guilty." The judge then fined the jurors for contempt. He had them held in jail until they paid the fines. Edward Bushel and three other jurors spent the next three months in jail. They appealed to a higher court and Parliament through a little-known *writ of habeas corpus*. Their appeals were granted, and they were freed.

For the next hundred years, written accounts of "The Trial of William Penn" and "Bushel's Case" (the appeal of the jurors), were widely published and read throughout Britain and its American colonies. They helped establish America's traditions of free speech, freedom of religion, "jury nullification," and writs of *habeas corpus*.

Cover Sheet of Published Pamphlet Describing the Trial of William Penn in London in 1670. This particular pamphlet was published by W.L. Mackenzie in England in 1630. Public Domain.

19.

Quakers buy half of New Jersey.

In 1671, George Fox, then 47 years old, travelled to America. He first sailed to the Caribbean island of Barbados. He spoke out against the mistreatment of African slaves he met there. He urged Quakers to invite slaves to their meeting house and worship together with them.

Fox then sailed to Maryland and visited Quakers there. He also met and preached to Protestants of all denominations, Catholics, and even Native Americans.

In May of 1672, Fox visited Quakers in New York and Long Island. He took part in their "Half-Year's Meeting" at Oyster Bay.

Fox thoroughly explored New Jersey along the way. He and other Quaker leaders rode on horseback from Maryland to New Castle, Delaware. From there, they and their horses took a small sailboat across the river to New Jersey. Fox and his party then made "a tedious journey" through "bogs, rivers, creeks, and wild woods" to Middletown. That was a new Quaker settlement on Sandy Hook Bay near Staten Island.

"Notable Audience in Maryland to Hear George Fox. The Founder of the Society of Friends or Quakers". Lithograph published by American School before 1923. Source: Wikimedia Commons as "George Fox Preaching in Maryland".

Fox observed that southern New Jersey was "not then inhabited by English so that we have travelled a whole day together, without seeing man or woman, house or dwelling place."

A Quaker from Middletown then took Fox and his party to the meeting at Oyster Bay on his sailboat.

On their way back to Maryland, Fox and his party traveled through different parts of New Jersey. They "hired Indians to help with their canoes." They "passed through many Indian towns, rivers, and bogs."

When Fox returned to England in 1673, he stayed at the home of William Penn and his wife, Gulielma, near London. There, he talked to them and other Quaker leaders about what he saw in New Jersey.

"They began to realise that this tract of land could become the Quaker homeland of their dreams. There they could put their vision freely into practice and show its strength to the world. Penn's connections could make this possible".[1]

George Fox also spoke with Edward Byllynge. Byllynge had met Fox and become a Quaker while a young cavalry officer for Parliament during the English Civil Wars. Byllynge later moved to London and became a successful merchant, brewer, and beer distributor. Byllynge was well known for openly defending Quakers against persecution. He had published several pamphlets urging Parliament to recognize and protect freedom of religion for all. Byllynge also knew and did business with Lord Berkeley.

In 1674, Byllynge bought Berkeley's undivided half-interest of New Jersey for 1,000 British Pounds (152,000 British Pounds today).

It was a complicated transaction. Byllynge was wealthy, but he owed many debts. To avoid title problems, Byllynge made John Fenwick, another wealthy Quaker, the legal owner of his purchase as his "trustee."

---

1   From *"Mission work and Quaker settlement in Colonial New Jersey"* (2025), Quakers in the World. https://www.quakersintheworld.org/quakers-in-action/280)

A Map of PENSILVANIA, NEW-JERSEY, NEW-YORK, And the THREE DELAWARE COUNTIES: By Lewis Evans. MDCCXLIX.
Published by Lewis Evans March 23 1749 according to Act of Parliament
Longitude from Philadelphia
A Scale of English Miles 60 to a Degree.
Explanation
PROVINCES. COUNTIES
CITIES. . Town. Villages & Camps
Forts . Carrying Places.
The Bounds of Pensilvania by Patent
L. Ontario
ONOYDAGES
ONON-DA-GAES
TUSCARORAES
MOHOCKS
ALBANY CO.
NEW-YORK
ULSTER CO.
DUTCHES CO.
PART OF CONECTICUT.
ORANGE
BERGEN CO.
MORRIS CO.
ESSEX
LONG I.
SUFFOLK CO.
The Sound
THE ENDLESS MOUNTAINS
Impenetrable Mountains
The blue Mountains
PART OF MARY LAND
PART OF VIRGINIA
CHESEPEAK BAY.
DELAWARE BAY.
DELAWARE COUNTIES
HUNTERDON
MONMOUTH
BURLINGTON
GLOUCESTER CO.
SALEM CO.
CUMBERLAND CO.
CAPE MAY CO.
THE ATLANTIC OCEAN.
Cape May
Susquehanna R.
Kats Kill Mts.
Remarks on the ENDLESS MOUNTAINS &c.
Allegeny Mountains
Longitude West from London

Byllynge divided his purchase into 100 shares. Each share was a "propriety" owned by a "proprietor." These proprietors did not own any particular parcel of land in New Jersey. They, along with George Carteret, owned an undivided share of the rights to sell all of that land.

They would not get title to a particular parcel until the land was surveyed and divided. Byllynge estimated that after the division, the owner of each share would own roughly 20,000 acres (31.25 square miles) of land.

Some investors bought many shares. Others bought fractions of shares as small as 1/16 and 1/32. Many borrowed money and mortgaged their shares. As a result, hundreds of investors and lenders owned some interest in New Jersey. Not all of them were Quakers.

In 1674, Byllynge and Fenwick had a dispute over what share each of them owned. They settled their differences through Quaker arbitrations. Fenwick ended up with 10%. Byllynge, his investors, and his creditors owned the remaining 90%. William Penn and three other Quakers replaced Fenwick as Byllynge's trustees.

In 1675, Fenwick led several hundred Quakers to New Jersey. They built a new settlement by the Delaware River. They named it "Salem," the Biblical English translation of the Hebrew word for peace.

William Penn, and the other three Quaker trustees stayed in London to work with George Carteret. He still owned most of the other half of New Jersey. In July

Image to left: "A Map of Pennsylvania, New Jersey, New York and Three Delaware Counties: By Lewis Evans, 1749." Britain established these four new colonies on territory it had taken from the Dutch, known as "New Netherland." In 1674, a group of Quakers purchased a one-half interest of New Jersey. In 1676, they and George Carteret, the owner of the other half, divided New Jersey into two separate colonies. The Quakers then took ownership and control of the half that became West New Jersey..

of 1676, the five of them agreed to divide and control it as two separate colonies. They wrote their agreement into the "Quintipartite" (Five Party) Deed.

The "Quintipartite Deed" of 1676 created a straight boundary line that ran from Little Egg Harbor in the south to a point by the Delaware Water Gap in the north. Carteret was to own all unsold land east of that line as "East New Jersey." Byllynge, Fenwick and the other Quakers would own everything west of that line as "West New Jersey."

The terms "East New Jersey" and "West New Jersey" are confusing today. That is because most of what began as "East New Jersey" is now known as "North Jersey." Most of what began as "West New Jersey" is now known as "South Jersey."

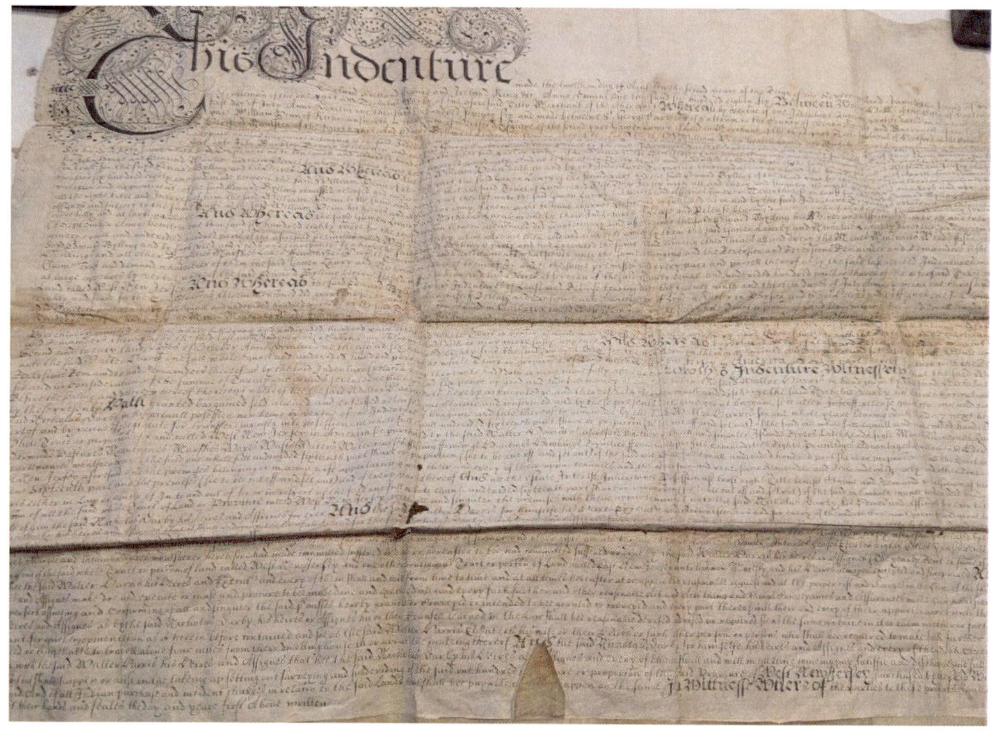

Deed by Walter Harris of Dublin to Nicholas Darby of Dublin dated August 12, 1686. It conveys 1/16 of "One Whole Full Equal and Undivided Hundred Part of the Whole Tract of Land Called West New Jersey in America". The Purchase Price Is: "21 Pounds, 17 Shillings, and 6 Pence." Source: Private Collection, Morristown, New Jersey.

20.

Quakers settle in Salem and Burlington. William Penn gives "West New Jersey" a constitution.

After agreeing with George Carteret to divide New Jersey, William Penn and Edward Byllynge worked to create a government for their West New Jersey. This was a complicated and uncertain process.

They first had to draft a new "Concession and Agreement" to govern their colony. They then had to get it approved by James, the Duke of York.

The original 1664 "Concessions" gave Berkeley and Carteret the right to rule New Jersey. While they were free to sell their land as they pleased, they had no authority to sell their right to run the government there.

Moreover, some British officials claimed that the brief Dutch conquest and occupation of New Jersey, and the treaty that returned it, wiped out all rights of Berkeley and Carteret. According to them, New Jersey was again under the complete control of James, Duke of York, as part of New York or "New England."

Penn, Byllynge and the other Quakers ignored those claims. They quickly drafted new "Concessions" to establish their own separate colonial government in West New Jersey. They then lobbied James to approve it.

Penn and Byllynge consulted with some of the most respected political thinkers in England. They included Algernon Sidney and John Locke.

John Locke claimed that each individual is born with certain "natural rights," and that "governments are instituted" to "secure" them. Locke said that societies are built on a "social contract" with which people create governments that "derive their just powers from the consent of the governed."

"Portrait of Algernon Sidney". Copy of 1663 Painting by Justus van Egnon. Source: National Trust, U.K. Posted by Wikimedia Commons. Public Domain.

Algernon Sidney added that the "just powers" of governments must be very limited. That is because their only purpose is to protect the freedom, safety, and property of each citizen.

The writings of John Locke and Algernon Sidney were later widely published throughout England and its colonies. America's Founders often referred to them when writing our Declaration of Independence and Constitution.

Penn and Byllynge were greatly influenced by Locke and Sidney. However, they were also influenced by the real-world experiences of Quakers living under colonial charters in Virginia, Massachusetts, Connecticut, and Maryland.

The new Concessions included much of what was written in 1664 Concessions by Berkeley and Carteret. However, they added other rights and details, including these:

1. No taxes can be imposed without the consent of an elected "Assembly".
2. "No person or persons… shall be… punished or hurt . . . for the sake of his opinion, judgment, faith or worship towards God. . ."
3. "No proprietor, freeholder or inhabitant of the said province of West New-Jersey, shall be deprived or condemned of life, limb, liberty, estate, property, or any ways hurt in his or their privileges, freedoms or franchises, upon any account whatsoever, without a due trial."
4. All civil and criminal trials shall be determined by 12-member juries. If an "Indian" (Native American) is a party to a case, six of the twelve jurors must be "Indians."
5. Voting in all elections must be by secret ballots placed in a sealed ballot box.
6. Ten "commissioners" elected each year will survey and divide the land. They will decide how specific parcels of land will be sold or distributed to the proprietors.
7. No land claimed by "Indians" can be sold unless they agree and are paid a fair price.

William Penn described his new charter as follows:

"We have made Concessions by ourselves, being such as Friends here and there (we question not) will approve of. . . There we lay a foundation for after ages to understand their liberty as men and Christians, that they may not be brought in bondage but with their own consent, for we put the power in the people."

Many of these rights are described and protected in the United States Constitution we have today.

However, William Penn, Edward Byllynge, and the other Quakers still had much work to do. James, Duke of York, had not yet agreed to let them set up a government in West New Jersey.

There were years of conflict, tension, and uncertainty. Edmund Andros, the Governor of New York, ordered his officials in nearby New Castle to inspect and collect taxes on all goods shipped to and from Quaker settlers in Salem. John Fenwick, the Quaker leader in Salem, claimed that Andros had no right to act in New Jersey. He urged Quakers there not to cooperate with any New York authorities. Andros had Fenwick arrested, taken to New York, jailed, fined, and released on at least two occasions.

In spite of this, in May of 1677, 230 Quakers bought land and built a second new settlement farther up the Delaware River. They named it "Burlington."

"Portrait of Sir Edmund Andros" by Mary Beale (1680). Andros fought for the King during the English Civil Wars and was fiercely loyal to King Charles II and his brother James afterwards. James appointed Andros to be Governor of New York from 1674 to 1680. During that time, Andros claimed that New Jersey was part of New York and under his control. Painting photographed by the Virginia Historical Society and posted in the Encyclopedia Virginia and Wikimedia Commons. Public Domain.

Many Native Americans lived there. Some sold their land to the Quakers and moved elsewhere. Their agreements and deeds were put in writing. Many show that the Native Americans knew the value of the land they sold

"Burlington Meeting House, 1687-1786" Illustration by J. Collins in 1900 "From an old painting". Published in Smithsonian Magazine 2017. Public Domain

and the goods they bought. In a typical deed, one Native American was paid the following goods for a section of woods he sold in Burlington in 1677:

"30 matchcoats, 20 guns, 30 kettles and one great one, 30 pair of hose, 20 fathom (120 feet) of duffelds (coarse wool fabric), 30 petticoats, 30 narrow hoes, 30 bars of lead, 15 small barrels of powder, 70 knives, 30 Indian axes, 70 combs, 60 pair of tobacco tongs, 60 scissars (sic), 60 tinshaw looking glasses (eyeglasses), 120 awl blades, 120 fish hooks, 2 grasps of red paint, 120 needles, 60 tobacco boxes, 120 pipes, 200 bells, 100 Jewsharps, and 6 anchors (60 gallons) of rum."[2]

---

2   Source: Smith, Samuel (1765). *The History of the Colony of Nova-Cæsaria, or New-Jersey, etc.* (WS Sharp, 1877) p. 95, https://archive.org/details/bim_eighteenth-century_the-history-of-the-colon_smith-samuel_1765

While this was going on, Penn, Byllynge, and other "Friends" stayed in London. There, they mastered the art of court intrigue and British politics. They won over many key officials and skillfully played powerful factions and personalities against each other. On August 6, 1680, James finally signed papers recognizing Quaker political control of West New Jersey. The new Concession and Agreement then took effect. In 1681, elections were held, and the first Assembly met in Burlington.

At some point, William Penn lost interest in West New Jersey. In 1681, King Charles II gave Penn land west of the Delaware River to satisfy a debt the King owed to Penn's father. Penn called it "Pennsylvania" or "Penn's Forests." In 1682, he arrived there to continue his "Holy Experiment." Penn began by planning and building a new city. He called it "Philadelphia," which means "Brotherly Love."

In 1683, William Penn made the "Treaty of Shackamaxon" with Tamanend, a chief of the Lenni Lenape. The two agreed in writing that Quakers and Lenni Lenape would "live in peace as long as the waters run in the rivers and creeks and as long as the stars and moon endure."

"The Treaty of Penn with the Indians". Painting by Benjamin West 1771. Source: Pennsylvania Academy of Fine Arts Philadelphia. Public Domain.

21.

Most Lenni Lenape leave New Jersey and move North and West.

Only about 8,000 to 10,000 Native Americans lived in what is now New Jersey when the first Europeans arrived. In 1623, the Dutch built a small fort by the Delaware River that they called Nassau (now Gloucester City, New Jersey). There, they traded with nearby Native Americans. During the 1630s, Swedes and Finns built a fort and settlement on the other side of the Delaware River that they called Cristiana (now Wilmington, Delaware). Over the next twenty years, more Swedes and Finns arrived. They built additional settlements nearby.

Soon afterwards, thousands of Native Americans living in what are now New Jersey, Pennsylvania, and Delaware died of smallpox and other diseases. This was roughly half of the Native American population there.

Many Native Americans who survived blamed the Swedes and Finns for "bringing evil amongst them." They said, "Many of the Indians since their coming were dead." They prepared for war to drive them out.

In 1654, John Printz, the Governor of the Swedes, heard of this. He set up a meeting with the "sachems" (chiefs) of many of the surrounding Native American communities. He denied doing anything to harm them or their people. Afterwards, one Lenape sachem, Noaman, defended the Swedes. He also "rebuked" those who "spoke evil" of them. He said that the Swedes were "good people." He said the Swedes had treated them fairly and given them "considerable presents." Most of the Lenni Lenape agreed with him. They made a treaty of friendship with the Swedes.

About 25 years later, Quakers in Burlington faced similar accusations and responded in a similar way. According to Thomas Budd, a Quaker leader and member of the Assembly,

"Johan Printz", Governor of New Sweden, 1643-1653. By Unknown Artist. Source: Wikimedia Commons. Public Domain

"The Indians told us, they were advised to make war on us, and cut us off whilst we were but a few. . .

"They were told, that we sold them the small-pox, with the mach (match) coat (an outer garment of coarse woolen cloth) they had bought of us. . . (This) caused our people to be in fears and jealousies concerning them; therefore we sent for the Indian Kings, to speak with them, who with many more Indians, came to Burlington, where we had a conference about the matter. . .

"(W)e told them that we came amongst them by their own consent, had bought the land off them which we honestly paid them for. . . And for what commodities we had bought at anytime of them, we had paid them for. . . (We) had been just to them, and had from the time of our first coming been very kind and respectful to them. Therefore we knew no reason why they had to make war on us;

"To which one of them. . . on behalf of the rest, made the following speech in answer:

"Our young men speak such words as we do not like, nor approve of, and we cannot help that. We are your brothers and intend to live like brothers with you. We have no mind to have war, we are only skin and bones. The meat that we eat doth not do us good. We always are in fear. We have not the benefit of the sun to shine on us. We hide us in holes and corners.

"If we intend at any time to make war on you, we will let you know of it, and the reasons why we make war on you. And if you make us satisfaction for the injury done us for which the war is intended, then we will not make war on you.

"And if you intend to make war on us, we would have you let us know of it, and the reasons for which you make war on us. And then if we do not make satisfaction, for the injury done unto you, then you may make war on us. Otherwise, you ought not to do it.

"You are our brothers, and we are willing to live like brothers with you. . .

"And as to the small-pox, it was in my grandfather's time, and it could not be the English that could send it us then. And it was once in my father's time, they could not send it then neither. And now it is in our time, and I do not believe they have sent it now. I do believe it is the Man Above that hath sent it us. . ."

At that time, nobody knew that many Europeans carried and spread germs that caused deadly diseases without knowing it. Those diseases included smallpox, measles, influenza, and cholera. They usually made Europeans only mildly sick or not sick at all. However, they were deadly to Native Americans.

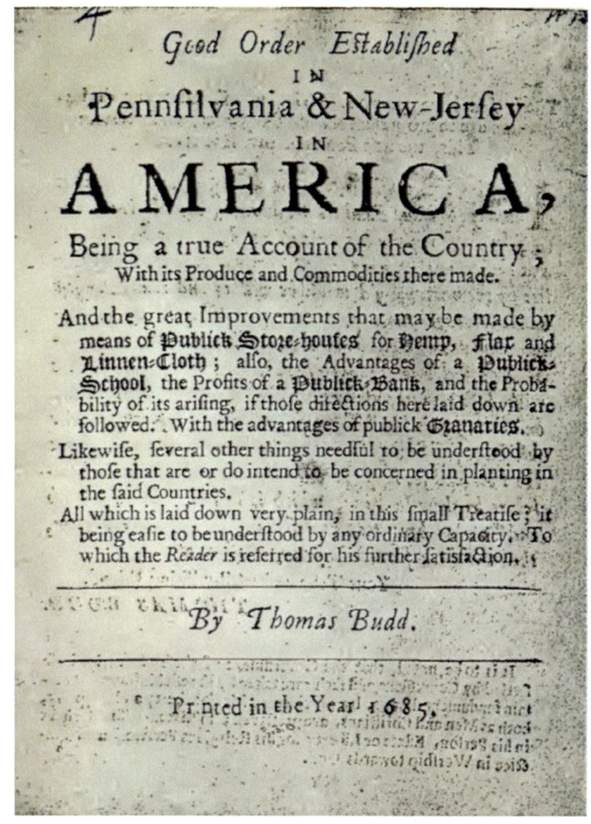

These diseases had been just as deadly to Europeans many years before. However, those who survived had an immunity that was passed on to their descendants.

Alcohol was also deadly to Native Americans. Their leaders begged the Quakers at Burlington not to sell their people "rum, brandy, and other strong liquors." They admitted being a people who "did not have government of themselves to drink them in moderation."

Ockanickon, an old and respected Native American "king," made this final plea to the Quakers of Burlington just before he died:

"Strong liquors were first sold us by the Dutch, and they were blind. They had no eyes. They did not see it was for our hurt. And the next people that came amongst us were the Sweeds, who continued the sale of those strong liquors to us. . . They were also blind. They had no eyes. They did not see it to be hurtful to us to drink it, although we know it to be hurtful to us."

"But if people will sell it to us, we are so in love with it that we cannot forbear it. When we drink it, it makes us mad. We do not know what we do. We then abuse one another. We throw each other into the fire. Seven score (140) of our people have been killed by reason of the drinking of it since the time it was first sold us. Those people that sell it, they are blind. . .

"But now there is a people come to live amongst us that have eyes. They see it to be for our hurt. And we know it to be for our hurt. They are willing to deny themselves of the profit of it for our good. These people have eyes. We are glad such a people are come amongst us. . ."

The Quakers in Burlington enacted many laws and tried to stop people in West New Jersey from selling alcohol to Native Americans. However, they were as ineffective as those who tried to prohibit the manufacture and sale of liquor in Atlantic City during the 1920s.

By 1755, very few Native Americans still lived in New Jersey. Some lived in the northwest by the Delaware Water Gap. A few hundred lived near Burlington. Some lived in mixed-race communities like Gouldtown in Cumberland County. However, most Lenape-speakers lived in Lenni Lenape communities like Wyoming in northern and western Pennsylvania, western New York State, and the Ohio Valley.

Between 1756 and 1758, bands of Lenni Lenape from there attacked and killed more than two dozen Whites in northwest New Jersey near the Delaware Water Gap.

The Governor and Legislature of New Jersey appointed "commissioners" to "examine" the cause of this violence. They met several times with Lenape-speaking leaders in Crosswicks, near Bordentown.

The Lenape leaders blamed Whites for the violence. Some said Native Americans had become violent after drinking liquor sold by Whites. Others told of Native Americans who claimed Whites had tricked them into signing away

"Defeat of General Braddock in the French and Indian War, in 1755" Engraving by John Andrew made in 1855. Source. Library of Congress via Wikimedia Commons. Public Domain.

their land. Some said Native Americans had attacked Whites who hunted, fished, or set dangerous traps on land they had not sold.

However, the most likely cause was the "French and Indian War" (also "The Seven Years' War"). France and its Native American allies had been fighting the British and their "colonials" in America since 1755. At first, the British suffered humiliating defeats in western Pennsylvania and New York. When the French were winning, many Native Americans attacked British settlers and helped the French.

One of them was a Lenni Lenape "sachem" (chief) named Teedyuscung. English settlers called him "King of the Delawares."

"Teedyuscung", 1750 Painting. Posted by Descendent Chris Eveland to Finda-grave.com on 09 Nov 2014

Teedyuscung was born around 1700 in what is now Trenton, New Jersey. He grew up around wealthy Whites there. Although fluent in English and several Indian languages, he supported himself by making and selling brooms and baskets. He and his family later moved to a Lenni Lenape community near Easton, Pennsylvania. Then they moved to Wyoming, Pennsylvania.

"Map of Pennsylvania with Shaded Area on Right as the Lands of the 'Walking Purchase.'" In 1736, the sons of William Penn claimed they had found a "lost" treaty from 1686 in which the Lenni Lenape agreed to sell certain land between the Delaware and Lehigh rivers. The land to be sold was "as far as a Man could walk in a day and a half." The document was probably forged. The Penn family then hired trained runners to run, rather than walk, for a day and a half. This forced the Lenni Lenape to sell roughly 1,200 square miles of their best land at far less than its value in 1737. [3]

---

3   This image is in the public domain because it came from the site https://www.demis.nl/products/web-map-server/examples/ and was released by the copyright holder. Permission is granted to copy, distribute and/or modify this map since it is based on free of copyright images from: www.demis.nl. See also approval email on de.wp and its clarification

William Penn died penniless in England in 1718. His three sons, Thomas, John, and Richard, then became the main proprietors of Pennsylvania. They did not share their father's Quaker ideals. They instead tried to squeeze as much money as they could out of their colony.

Teedyuscung was a powerful and persuasive speaker. Many Lenni Lenape clans chose him to be their chief. Teedyuscung repeatedly denounced the "Walking Purchase."

When the French and Indian War began, Teedyuscung led deadly raids against English settlers. However, in 1757, he worked to make peace with them.

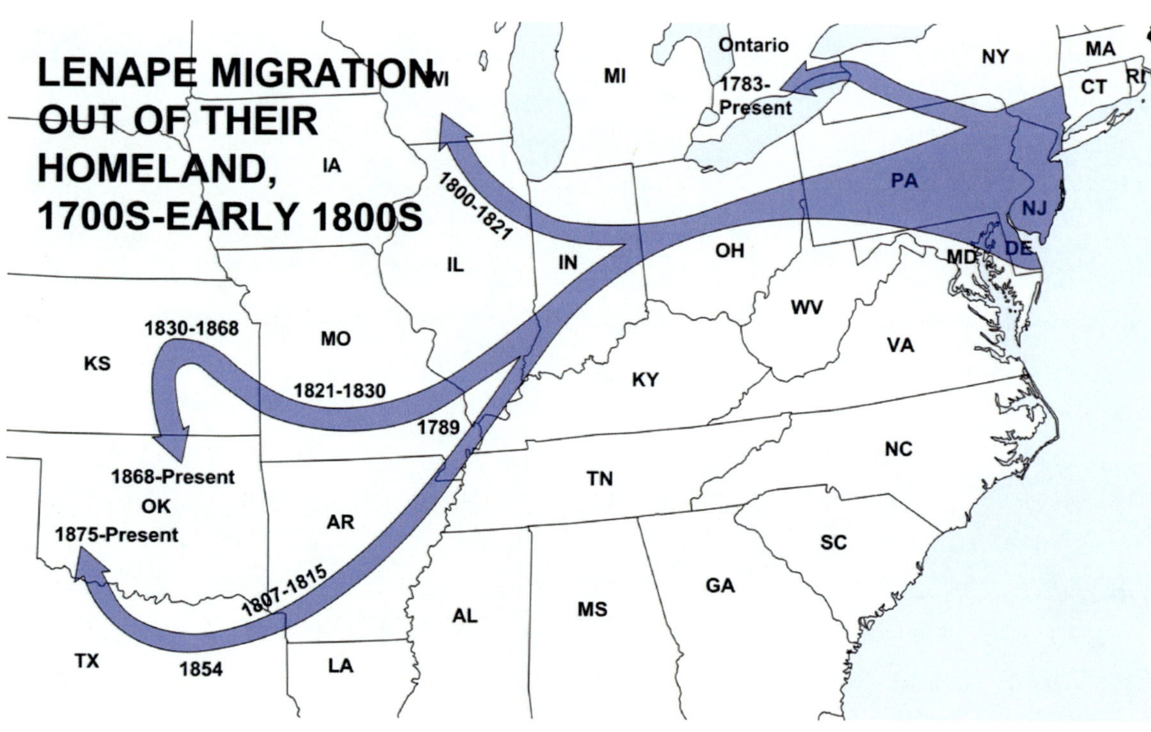

Map of "Lenape Migration Out of their Homeland, 1700s-Early 1800s." Reprinted from **West Windsor History Book** *published by Historical Society of West Windsor, N.J. and* **The Lenape: Archaeology, History and Ethnography,** *New Jersey Historical Society: Edition I (1986) by Herbert C. Kraft.*

At that time, the British army and colonial militias were getting stronger and beginning to win battles.

In October of 1758, Teedyuscung helped arrange for himself and the chiefs of 12 other nations to negotiate peace with representatives from New Jersey and Pennsylvania. They met near Easton. About five hundred other Native Americans and a delegation of Quakers also attended.

After 18 days, they reached several agreements that were written into the "Treaty of Easton."

In it, the Native Americans agreed to stop attacking English soldiers and settlers. They also agreed to stop helping the French. This was a critical turning point of the French and Indian War. It isolated and doomed French Canada.

Several Lenni Lenape-speaking nations also agreed to leave New Jersey and move west. In return, New Jersey paid them "1,000 Spanish Dollars." Pennsylvania guaranteed them full ownership and control of large areas of land in Western Pennsylvania and the Ohio River Valley.

In a later agreement, New Jersey bought five acres of land for some 200 Christian Lenape-speakers who still lived near Burlington. That settlement was called Brotherton. Today it is known as Indian Mills. Later, some Nanticoke and other Algonquians who lived near the Chesapeake Bay also moved there.

By 1802, there were only a few dozen Native Americans in Brotherton. They sold their land and moved near Oneida Lake by Syracuse, New York. In 1824, they moved to new land they bought near Lake Michigan.

In 1832, several elderly Lenni-Lenape leaders approached the New Jersey Legislature. They asked the state to buy their hunting and fishing rights on public land in New Jersey that they were no longer using. The Legislature agreed and paid them $2,000.

Descendants of those Lenni-Lenape speaking nations today live in Wisconsin, Kansas, Oklahoma, and Delaware. Some also live in Ontario, Canada.

Current webpage of the Oklahoma Headquarters of the Delaware Tribal Government. Many Lenni-Lenape also call their tribe the Delaware.

22.

Americans break "The Treaty of Easton." A Lenape preacher inspires "Pontiac's War."

The last French army in Canada surrendered to the British on September 8, 1760. When that happened, many Americans from Connecticut to Virginia moved to the Ohio River Valley. They settled on land that Pennsylvania had given to the Lenni Lenape in the Treaty of Easton.

Neolin was a Lenni Lenape who lived there. In 1761, he claimed that God, the "Master of Life," had spoken to him in a vision. For two years, he traveled from village to village throughout Pennsylvania, the Ohio Valley, and the Great Lakes region. Neolin spoke of his vision to many Native Americans from many nations.

Neolin said that the Master of Life was displeased with them for becoming immoral and adopting the ways of Whites.

Neolin urged them to "purify" themselves. He told them to return to traditional ways. He told them not to "drink to the point of madness." He told

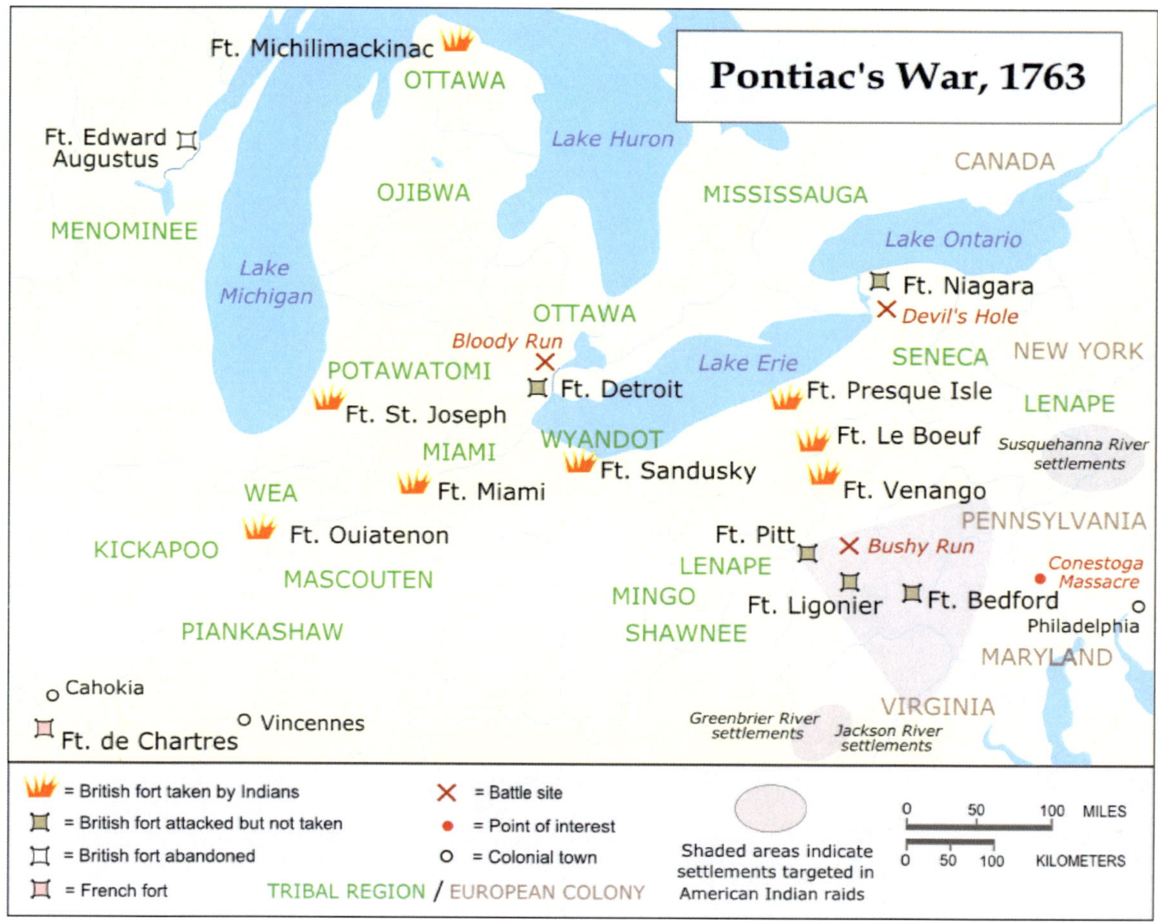

"Forts and Battles of Pontiac's War 1763". Meyers, Kevin, (2009), Permission GNU Free Documentation License. Posted on Wikimedia.com

them not to "fight one another." He instructed men to "have only one wife and do not chase after the wives of others." He called on them to "make war" against Whites and "drive them from our lands."

Pontiac was chief of the Ottawas. They were a nation of Algonquians who lived along the shores of Lake Huron. Pontiac preached Neolin's message to Native Americans there. He urged them to unite in a war to drive out the Whites.

On April 19, 1763, Teedyuscun, the Lenape chief, was murdered in his home in Wyoming, Pennsylvania.

"Proclamation Line of 1763" (captions in German). Author: Nikater. Released by copyright holder to public domain.

One week later, Pontiac led thousands of warriors from many nations into war against the British. In May and June of 1763, they attacked and overran eight British forts between the Ohio River and Lake Michigan. They surrounded four others, including Detroit and Fort Pitt (Pittsburgh). Pontiac and his Native American allies killed hundreds of British and American soldiers, traders, and settlers. However, they failed to drive out the British.

Pontiac's War ended after the summer. The British promised to enforce the Treaty of Easton. On October 7, 1763, King George III issued a Proclamation. It barred all British subjects from entering Native American lands west of the Appalachian Mountains without permission. These included the lands in the Ohio River Valley promised to the Lenni Lenape (Delaware). It also barred colonial governments from approving or recording titles for land there. The King's Cabinet sent 10,000 soldiers to keep settlers out of Native American lands. Parliament agreed to spend 250,000 British Pounds per year to maintain those troops.

This angered many Americans. They believed their colonial militias had driven out the French. They thought they had won the right to settle in the lands they had conquered. They did not know how Teedyuscung, the Lenni Lenape, and the Treaty of Easton had helped make their victory possible.

This anger caused many Americans to demand independence from Britain twelve years later.

23.

John Somers builds a log house near the "Point" where the river meets the Great Egg Harbor.

Around 1680, a 32-year-old Quaker named John Somers left England and bought land north of where William Penn later built Philadelphia. A few years later, he married Hannah Hodgkin. He then bought a tract of uninhabited woods in West New Jersey by the Atlantic Ocean. It was near the north "point" of where a large river flowed into the back bay called Great Egg Harbor.

That harbor had been named by Cornelius Jacobsen Mey, a Dutch merchant and ship's captain. He had seen large quantities of eggs from wild birds in the surrounding marshes when he sailed there during June of 1614. He then named the bay "Eyren Haven." That is Dutch for "Eggs Harbor."

English settlers later called it "Great Egg Harbor." They named the deep-water river that ran into it the "Great Egg Harbor River." They called a back bay 20 miles to the north "Little Egg Harbor". They called its river the "Little Egg Harbor River." Later, they called it the "Mullica River" after Eric Mullica.

"Caerte vande Suydt Rivier in Niew Nederland" (Map of South River in New Netherland" made in 1639. It identified "Eyren Eylandt" (Island of Eggs) and "Eyren Haven" (Harbor of Eggs) in the lower right-hand corner.

Eric Mullica had left Sweden with his family in 1654. They lived in one of several settlements along the Delaware River that were part of a Swedish colony called "New Sweden." When the Dutch and British seized that colony, he moved to New Jersey. There, he built a farm by the Little Egg Harbor River in what is now Mullica Township.

John Somer's land by the Great Egg Harbor was well-suited for both farming and trade. Besides having rich soil, it had access to excellent deep-water transportation. Somers could easily sail up the river to Mays Landing. He could sail through protected back bays as far north as Little Egg Harbor and as far south as Cape May. Ships sailing on the ocean between New York and Philadelphia often stopped at the harbor to seek shelter from storms. They also often stopped to buy fresh eggs and produce from local farmers.

The log house built by Thomas Shinn, a Quaker, in Burlington in 1712. During the 1690s, John Somers and his wife Hannah built a similar log house on the hill in Somers Point where the "Somers Mansion" stands today. Photo from Historic American Building Survey (HABS), Library of Congress. Public Domain.

Sketch of Quaker Meeting House built in Somers Point in 1695. Based on recollection of Deborah Jane Somers Anderson for Stewart's Geneology and Miscellany c. 1918. Pp.33-34. Source: 300 Years at the Point by William Kelly.

John and Hannah Somers burned trees and cleared land for a farm. They built a log house on a hill overlooking the bay. In 1693, John Somers began a ferry service to and from Beesley's Point across the Great Egg Harbor River. He carried people, livestock, and goods on an open boat with oars and sails.

Families named Adams, Covenhoven (later Conover), Gilbert, Scull, Steelman, and Valentine settled nearby. Other families named Adams, Gale, Higbee, Ireland, Lake and Risley arrived later.

Most were Quakers. Covenhoven, Scull and Valentine came from Long Island in the former Dutch colony of New Netherland. Although the British now ruled it, Quakers were still persecuted there.

In 1695, Quakers or "Friends" living in the area built a meeting house for worship. It stood on what is now a corner of New York Avenue and Shore Road.

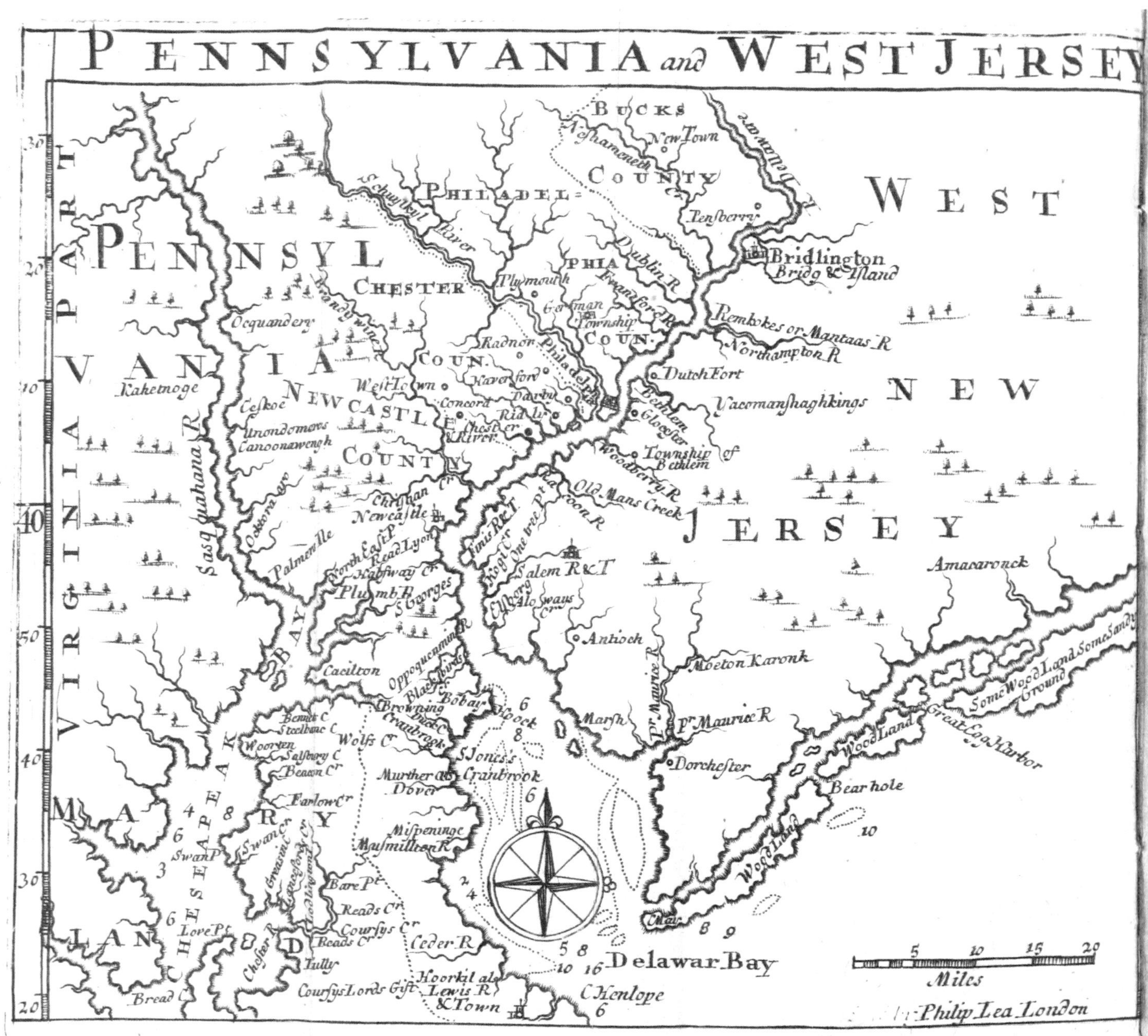

"Map of Pennsylvania and West Jersey" published by Gabriel Thomas in 1698 shows Great Egg Harbor below an island of "Some Woodland-Some Sandy Ground" by the lower right-hand corner.

24.

Somers and his neighbors
enjoy prosperous, comfortable lives.

John Somers and his neighbors built sturdy houses for themselves. They built barns and pens for their horses, cows, goats, pigs, and sheep. They also built boats.

Their farms were surrounded by forests of "working timber." There were abundant "oak, ash, chestnut, pine, cedar, poplar, and fir" trees. They were suitable for building anything from furniture to large ships.

They used boats to bring their livestock to graze on the grass of islands in the back bays and on barrier islands along the ocean. One island between Somers Point and Ocean City is still known as Cowpens Island.

They found deposits of clay to make bricks for foundations, fireplaces, and chimneys.

John Somers and his neighbors planted corn, beans, squash, and potatoes in their fields like the Native Americans. They also dug up clams and oysters and used nets to catch fish in the back bays and tidal creeks. They gathered eggs from nesting birds along the shore. They hunted game and gathered wild fruits, nuts, and berries in the woods.

However, unlike the Native Americans, European settlers also planted rows of apple, pear, peach, and cherry trees. They often made cider and liquor from the juice of these fruits.

Colonial Family Working Together. Unknown 19th-century artist. Courtesy of the New Jersey Museum of Agriculture's Dow Brown Collection, New Brunswick. From New Jersey in the American Revolution by Barbara J. Mitnick.

25.

Daniel Coxe applies his "curious" mind to science, medicine and business.

As a young man, Daniel Coxe was described as a "curious" and "inquisitive" English scientist. In 1665, he was elected to the "Royal Society of London" at age 25. The "Royal Society" was dedicated to scientific inquiry and research. Astronomer (and later architect) Christopher Wren and chemistry pioneer Robert Boyle were among its founders. It was chartered by King Charles II in 1660. Some of the greatest scientists in England were members. Sir Isaac Newton became its President in 1703.

Coxe first did experiments and applied scientific methods to medicine. During the deadly plague in London in 1665, most respected physicians and "apothecaries" (pharmacists) used medicines made from tobacco. Coxe claimed that tobacco was a poison that did nothing to cure patients. To prove his point, he did a sensational experiment at a meeting of the Royal Society. He killed "a lusty cat" with an oil made from tobacco. Coxe claimed that most doctors were frauds.

"Portrait of Christopher Wren" (1711) by Godfrey Kneller, Library of Congress vis Wikimedia Commons. Public Domain.

"Portrait of the Honorable Robert Boyle: (1627-1691) by Johann Kerseboom. Source: Wellcome Collection via Wikimedia Commons. Creative Commons Attribution 4.0 International License.

John Locke was also a doctor and a scientist as a young man. He joined the Royal Society in 1668 and became friends with Coxe. Locke later became famous for his political theories.

In 1673 and 1674 Dr. Coxe did research and experiments to make "smelling salts." He extracted "volatile salts" from various plants. In 1675, Coxe wrote a study on growing plants in sea sand. That was his last published research with the Royal Society. After that, Daniel Coxe applied his curiosity, talent, and scientific methods to business.

During the 1670s, Coxe studied the Silk Road caravans that connected Mediterranean and Black Sea ports with China and the East. Italian merchants profited

Portrait of John Locke (1632-1704) by Herman Vereist. Source: National Portrait Gallery (UK) via Wikimedia Commons. Public Domain.

from that trade before the Ottoman Turks stopped them during the 1400s.

The Turks were often at war with most Italian states and their ally Spain. However, Spain was also an enemy of England. Daniel Coxe reasoned that since England and the Ottomans had common enemies, they could do business with each other.

After 1675, Daniel Coxe became a "wholesale merchant" for two Mediterranean shipping companies. He hoped to profit from the Silk Road trade.

Coxe was probably disappointed. The English had competition from Dutch and French merchants who were also enemies of Spain. His English ships probably had to pay tribute to avoid attacks by Barbary corsairs. Overland caravans to China and the East were less efficient than Dutch, Portuguese, and Spanish ships using southern sea routes.

However, Coxe probably realized that he could earn far more money from business than from science or medicine. He also acquired skills and made contacts that led him to better opportunities in America.

26.

Daniel Coxe's religion and politics are dangerous in England, but welcome in New Jersey.

Coxe did not support the "established" (government-run and funded) Church of England. Supporters of the King disapproved of this. They later called Coxe a "conventicler" or "dissenter". This made Coxe a well-known outsider like William Penn, Edward Byllynge, and other prominent Quakers.

Coxe also supported members of Parliament who later became known as "Whigs." They wanted to limit the power of King Charles II and his brother James. They accused both royals of using government appointments, permits, and contracts to buy votes in Parliament. They also feared that King Charles II and James were trying to restore the Catholic Church and rule Britain as absolute monarchs.

During this time, Daniel Coxe remained friends with John Locke. Both lived in the same neighborhood as the Earl of Shaftesbury, a leading Whig in Parliament. The three often talked about politics with others at the nearby Swan Tavern.

In 1679, King Charles II dismissed Parliament three times. Some 18,000 British subjects signed a petition urging the King to let Parliament do its business. Daniel Coxe was one of them.

Before they were submitted, the King issued a "Proclamation Against Tumultous Petitions." It ordered British subjects:

"not to Agitate or Promote any such Subscriptions, nor in any wise joyn in any Petition of that manner to be Preferred to His Majesty, upon Peril of the utmost Rigour of the Law that may be inflicted for the same."

In 1681, Shaftesbury was arrested and charged with treason. Although a jury acquitted him, Shaftesbury fled to Holland. John Locke also fled there two years later.

THE
Arraignment, Tryal & Condemnation
OF
Algernon Sidney, Esq;
FOR
High-Treason.
For Conspiring the Death of the
KING,
AND
Intending to raise a Rebellion in this
KINGDOM.
Before the Right Honourable
Sir GEORGE JEFFREYS, Knight and Baronet, Lord Chief Justice of England, at His Majesties Court of Kings-Bench at Westminster, on the 7th. 21th. and 27th. of November, 1683.
LONDON,
Printed for Benj. Tooke at the Ship in St. Paul's Church-Yard, 1684.

"The Arraignment, Tryal and Condemnation of Algernon Sidney, Esq. for High Treason, etc." Cover Sheet of Record of Court Proceedings Published in 1683

Algernon Sidney was the political philosopher who had helped William Penn and Edward Byllynge write their new "Concessions" for West New Jersey in 1676. Sidney was also an outspoken Whig who worked closely with Shaftesbury and Locke. In 1683, King Charles II ordered the arrest of Algernon Sidney and the search of his house.

Agents of the King found and seized unpublished notes Sidney had written explaining his theories on government and law. In them, Sidney had claimed that kings derived their authority from the people they governed. He had also written that people could lawfully resist and depose tyrants who violated a nation's fundamental laws.

Those papers were used to try, convict, and execute Algernon Sidney for treason six months later. In 1685, Charles II died. Parliament chose his brother James, Duke of York, to be King. James was Catholic. However, Charles II had a well-liked, illegitimate son who was a Protestant. He was known by his title, the Duke of Monmouth.

The Beheading of the Duke of Monmouth in London in 1685. Print from engraving by Jan Luyken in 1689. Public Domain

Soon after James became King, the Duke of Monmouth returned from Holland. He then led a "pitchfork" rebellion against his uncle to become King. He failed. The Duke of Monmouth and more than 400 of his followers were executed. Another 800 were sold as indentured servants to do ten years' hard labor with slaves in Barbados. Other supporters fled to America.

Monmouth County was created in East New Jersey in 1683. Some said it was to honor the Duke of Monmouth before his rebellion. Others denied ever naming their county after such a traitor.

King James then ordered the arrest of everyone in England who was "disaffected to the government." Daniel Coxe was arrested, but later released.

At that same time, King Louis XIV began persecuting Protestants (Huguenots) in France. Many of them contacted fellow Protestants in England to find places to live in America.

In 1685, Daniel Coxe was asked by an English friend to help him buy land in West New Jersey. His friend told Coxe that he and many others were preparing to "fly thither from the then approaching storm."

"The Trial of the Honourable Colonel Algernon Sidney, 1683." Painting by F.P. Stephanoff, in 1835. Source: Library of Congress via Wikimedia Commons. Public Domain.

27.

Daniel Coxe owns a million acres of land in West New Jersey.

Daniel Coxe met Edward Byllynge in either 1683 or 1684. At that time, the 60-year-old Byllynge was having a dispute with the estate of George Carteret who had died in 1679. Byllynge owned most land in West New Jersey. Carteret's estate owned most of East New Jersey.

Byllynge claimed that the 1676 boundary line between East and West New Jersey was inaccurate and had to be corrected. Byllynge said the parties intended that East and West New Jersey have roughly the same size and value. However, the maps they used proved to be wildly inaccurate. West New Jersey had far less land and far more "useless bogs." Byllynge demanded that the boundary line be moved farther north to enlarge West New Jersey.

In either 1683 or 1684, Byllynge bought shares of East New Jersey to increase his bargaining power. Daniel Coxe loaned Byllynge much of the money he needed. Coxe secured his loans by taking back mortgages on land and proprietary shares owned by Byllynge in both East and West New Jersey.

Previously described Deed by Walter Harris of Dublin to Nicholas Darby of Dublin dated August 12, 1686. It conveys 1/16 of "One Whole Full Equal and Undivided Hundred Part of the Whole Tract of Land Called West New Jersey in America". It recites that Harris had purchased this Share from "Daniel Gay" who had bought it from "Daniel Cox of London, Doctor in Physick" on July 30, 1684. Source: Private Collection, Morristown, New Jersey.

Later, Coxe became an owner. He foreclosed on some land and proprietary shares when Byllynge was unable to pay. In 1685 or 1686, Coxe also bought ownership from Byllynge of one proprietary share in East New Jersey and five in West New Jersey.

Coxe also reached out to other proprietors of East and West New Jersey and bought their shares. When Edward Byllinge died in 1687, Coxe bought most of the shares owned by his estate.

This made Coxe the largest proprietary owner of West New Jersey. In 1688, Coxe sent an agent to Burlington to survey the land and take ownership of specific tracts that he wanted. Coxe later hired other agents to buy more land in West Jersey from other proprietors and directly from Native Americans.

Name		Grantee / Other Party	Bk	Pg	Date	Location / Notes
COXE, Charles	fr	Coxe, William	I	67	9 16 1766	Sundry Tracts, Sussex
Charles	to	Coxe, William	I	73	9 16 1766	Sussex
Charles	fr	Henry, Samuel	A-E	385	7 28 1766	Bethlehem, Hunterdon
Charles	to	Paxton, James	A-E	390	10 29 1772	
Daniel ux,John& William	to		N	31-42	3 5 1746	Deed of Partition, Maps, Hunterdon & Morris
Daniel Estate	to	Akers, John	K	185	1 1 1749	Hopewell & Maidenhead, Hunterdon
Daniel	to	Allen, John	E-P	40	4 9 1734	Mt. Carmel, Hunterdon
Daniel	fr	Allen, John ux	G-H	453	4 9 1743	(SeeSec6Dr2),Mansfield, Burlington
Daniel	fr	Allen, John by Shrf	U	69	7 1 1764	Trenton, Hunterdon
Daniel	fr	Allen, William	E-P	402	8 2 1734	Trenton, Hunterdon
Daniel	to	Anderson, John	M	368	11 24 1733	Hunterdon
Daniel	fr	Anderson, John ux	E-P	400	11 24 1733	Trenton, Hunterdon
Daniel	fr	Bartlett, Benjamin ux	M	8,9	2 17 1686	
			M	25,26	2 18 1686	
Daniel	fr	Bartlett,Benjamin,Byllings, Loveday,West,Robert	M	8,10	2 25 1686	
			M	140,142	2 26 1686	
Daniel	fr	Bartlett, Benjamin ux	M	8,9,70	11 10 1688	Quit Claim
Daniel	fr	Bartlett, Benjamin Estate	E-P	370	9 12 1728	
Danie.John,Wm.	to	Beaumont, John	E-P	520	7 30 1743	Unappropriated Land
Daniel	fr	Bird, Daniel ux	E-P	374	2 12 1729	Sundry Tracts above Falls of Delaware
Daniel	fr	Browne,John,Sanders,Thomas	M	8,10	7 12 1687	
			M	144,146	7 13 1687	
Daniel	fr	Budd, Thomas	B	233	2 22 1688	Relative to Partition Line
Daniel	fr	Budd, Thomas	E-P	388	9 28 1689	Unappropriated Land
Daniel	to	Bull, Richard	Glo A	84	6 1 1713	Gloucester (City), Gloucester
Daniel	to	Burr, Henry	D-D	216	4 11 1733	Qt.Cl, Amwell, Hunterdon
Daniel	to	Burt, Joseph	E	322	6 8 1736	Hopewell, Hunterdon
Daniel	fr	Byllynge, Loveday	M	8,9	2 24 1686	
			M	65,67	2 25 1686	
Daniel	fr	Byllings, Edward	M	8,9	2 29 1683	
			M	61,62	3 1 1683	
Daniel	fr	Byllings, Edward	M	8,10	1 8 1685	
			M	133,135	1 9 1685	
Daniel	fr	Byllings, Edward	M	8,12	3 19 1685	
			M	257,259	3 20 1685	
Daniel	fr	Cadwalader, Thomas ux	T	4	7 1 1762	Maidenhead, Hunterdon
Daniel	to	Clinton, Hugh, Trustees	E	361	6 29 1738	
Daniel ux	to	Coldham, John	E-P	239	12 11 1691	Sundry Tracts above Falls of Delaware, Cape May
			E-P	240	12 12 1691	
Daniel	fr	Coldham, John	E-P	249	8 23 1692	Sundry Tres aboveFallsDelaware,CapeMay
Daniel Devisees	to	Coul, Christian	O	83	5 18 1757	Amwell, Hunterdon
Daniel	to	Coxe, Grace	Q	427	5 8 1761	Unappropriated Land
Daniel	to	Coxe, Grace	A-V	315	10 20 1765	Philipsburgh, Sussex
Daniel Estate	to	Coxe,John,Wm,Rebecca,Charles	I-K	164	11 2 1748	Partition of Lands,Map pg.172,Amwell, Hunterdon
Daniel	to	Dagworthy,John,Biles,Daniel	I-K	358	12 9 1751	Maidenhead & Hopewell, Hunterdon
Daniel,Rebecca, DanielJr,Grace &Charles	fr	Coxe,William,Saltar,Richard, Hooper, Robert L.	O	70	11 1 1757	Sundry Tracts, Hopewell, Hunterdon
Daniel	fr	Coxe, William	Q	272	11 15 1760	Kingwood, Hunterdon
Daniel	to	Coxe, William	Q	425	5 6 1761	Unappropriated Land
Daniel	to	Coxe,William & Grace	T	133	10 1 1761	Sussex
Daniel & Grace	fr	Coxe, William	R	254	2 1 1762	On Pequase River, Sussex

One of Many Pages of List of Deeds Recorded in New Jersey by Daniel Coxe and his Heirs. Source: Documents--The New Jersey Colonial Conveyances-1660-1780. https://westjerseyhistory.org/docs/cc/index.shtml

By 1690, Coxe owned roughly a million acres of land in West Jersey. He owned large tracts of land along the Delaware River, both north and south of Trenton. He owned almost all of what is now Cape May County. Coxe also owned land in East New Jersey. Coxe made large profits selling that land. Coxe also bought large tracts of land in other British colonies and tried to get grants of land as far as the Gulf of Mexico and the Mississippi River.

However, Daniel Coxe also wanted to build and run industries.

28.

Daniel Coxe builds "whale fishing," pottery and shipbuilding industries in West New Jersey without leaving England.

During the 1630s, Dutch and Swedish settlers near what is now Lewes, Delaware, saw many whales in Delaware Bay during late winter and early spring. They approached them with small boats, killed them with harpoons, and towed the carcasses to shore. There, they salted the meat, boiled the blubber to make oil, and used the bones to make various products. They found this work to be very profitable.

Daniel Coxe learned about "whale fishing" when he was an active member of the Royal Society. Between 1667 and 1668, it did research on "whale-fishing by the Bermudas" and "between the coast of New England and New Netherland."

Coxe made use of that research nearly twenty years later. After he bought land in West New Jersey, Coxe set up a whaling operation near Cape May. In 1686

Unknown Artist's Depiction of Hunting a Whale from a Small Boat. From Undated Postcard.

or 1687, he hired men to build buildings and boats at Town Bank. His agents hired crews from Long Island and elsewhere to be whalers for him in Delaware Bay. Coxe also invested in businesses to make various products from whales, market them, and ship them throughout the world.

To support his whaling operations, Coxe helped build a grist mill to grind grain into flour for his workers and their families. He helped build a sawmill to cut logs into lumber for his boats and buildings. The wheels of both mills were turned by tidal currents.

Coxe set up a "white pottery" business in Burlington. His agents built and operated kilns and workshops there. They produced high-quality dishes, cups, and other china. They marketed and sold them throughout several British colonies.

Cox also set up shipyards in Burlington. He built large and small ships. He also planned and started other businesses to supply his new industries with raw materials.

Coxe used his lands north of Trenton to buy and sell skins from beavers that Native Americans had hunted and trapped as far away as Canada.

Coxe also dominated the politics of West New Jersey. The Proprietors made him Governor of West New Jersey in 1687 and 1688 and again from 1689 to 1692.

"A Whale Female and the Windlass Whereby the Whales Are Brought Onshore". Illustration by Unknown Artist in Book Published by Awnsham and John Churchill in London in 1745.

During all this time, Coxe never left England. He hired agents to manage his businesses. He appointed Deputy Governors to run the colony.

Daniel Coxe had remarkable talent, energy, and discipline. However, he could not have achieved this level of success without the morals, ethics, and legal system that the Quakers had established in West New Jersey.

In 2002, a Chinese economist named Zhao Xiao explained this in a research paper that caused a sensation in Communist China. It was called "Market Economies With Churches and Market Economies Without Churches." In it, Xiao concluded that America's extraordinary commercial success was caused by its Christian morality. He claimed that most Americans in business did what was right because they wanted to, and not because the government forced them to. He claimed that China would enjoy more economic success if its Communist Party encouraged Christians instead of persecuting them.

In 1692, Coxe sold most of his land and businesses in West New Jersey to the West New Jersey Society. It was a joint-stock company owned by 48 London investors. Most of them later sold their stock to others. However, Cox still controlled much of its business through his son, Col. Daniel Coxe (also Daniel Coxe III).

Zhao Xiao during interview by Front-Line/World, an investigative documentary TV program and website distributed by PBS circa 2005.

The younger Col. Daniel Coxe moved to West New Jersey around 1689 and actively managed his father's business interests. In 1707, he married Sarah Eckley, the daughter of a prominent Quaker in Philadelphia. The couple eloped because the younger Coxe was a member of the Church of England. They lived at "Coxe Hall Creek Manor" in Cape May for many years. They then moved to Burlington.

Daniel Cox IV was the son of Col. Daniel Coxe and grandson of Dr. Daniel Coxe. In 1731, he claimed that the deeds to many properties sold by his father's West Jersey Society were defective. He claimed that he had inherited them. He then filed lawsuits to gain legal ownership of hundreds of properties from people who had bought land from the West New Jersey Society years before. Most of that land had been transformed from empty woods into valuable buildings and productive farms.

Although the claims of Daniel Cox IV were dubious, a 12-member jury and most judges ruled in his favor. The courts then forced hundreds of families to either repurchase their properties or be evicted. This caused enormous hardship. Many accused the judges and jurors of taking bribes. There were lawsuits, appeals, and riots. Images of Daniel Coxe IV were publicly burned, and his agents were threatened. Many who lost their homes in Hopewell in Burlington (now Mercer) County moved to the Yadkin Valley in North Carolina to start their lives over. That area became known as "The Jersey Settlement."

This method of fraud and abuse (or corruption) of the legal system by the great-grandson of Daniel Coxe was much like that of the "Walking Purchase" scam used by the sons of William Penn to steal the Lehigh River Valley from the Lenni Lenapi in 1737.

29.

John Townsend comes for freedom. Most Long Island whalers come to Cape May for land.

John Townsend was born in Oyster Bay, Long Island, around 1656. At that time, it was part of the Dutch colony of New Netherland. Its Governor, Peter Stuyvesant, persecuted Quakers who had settled there.

Townsend's parents and other family members defended their Quaker neighbors. In 1657, at least two of them (John Townsend and Henry Townsend) signed the "Flushing Remonstrance." It was a petition addressed to Dutch authorities. It demanded freedom of religion for all denominations of Christians and all non-Christians, including Jews. The Dutch threatened, banished, or arrested everyone who signed it.

Persecution of Quakers in Long Island continued even after the English took over in 1664. Around 1690, the younger John Townsend was arrested for allowing Quakers to meet and worship at his house. To avoid punishment, he moved to Cape May in West New Jersey.

During that same time, Peter Covenhoven (later Conover) and John Scull also left Long Island and moved near John Somers by Great Egg Harbor. That was

"Flushing Remonstrance of 1657". "John Townsend" and "Henry Townsend" are among the signers on the last page. Source: New York State Archives.

when the grandfather of Richard Stockton, who later signed the Declaration of Independence, moved from Long Island to Princeton in Burlington County.

John Townsend settled in Town Bank. There, he took part in the shore whaling operation set up by Daniel Coxe.

Later, Townsend donated land to build a Quaker meeting house in Town Bank. He then moved near what is now known as Townsend's Inlet between Sea Isle City and Avalon.

"Shore Whaling" by Cape May was difficult and dangerous. Whales only came there during the coldest months of the year. Whalers chased them in small open boats in rough seas and freezing weather. Then they had to tow the carcasses to shore and butcher them on the beach.

Quakers dominated the whaling industry in Nantucket and New Bedford in Massachusetts. However, few whalers who came to Cape May were Quakers seeking religious freedom like John Townsend. Most were Dutch, French, Swedish or English who came for cheap land. Some were Native Americans who had remained in the area. They supported themselves from farming during the summer when few, if any, whales were around.

One whaler, Chris Leaming, owned only 12 acres in Long Island. However, he bought 200 acres in Cape May. Shamgar Hand left 40 acres in Long Island to buy 500 acres in Cape May. Arthur Cresse had 30 acres in Long Island. He bought 350 acres in Cape May. Besides growing grain, these "yeoman whalers" also kept herds of cattle. Many of them also bought and owned black slaves.

Few Quakers owned slaves. However, in 1738, only 50 of the 1,200 inhabitants of Cape May County were Quakers. Quaker opposition to slavery was one of many issues that caused friction between political leaders in Cape May County and those in Burlington, Gloucester, and Salem counties where Quakers had far more influence.

By the 1750s, the massive shore whaling industry at Cape May had ended. Lew Cresse, a shore whaler from Cape May wrote then that, "After being out on the water for two months, we never saw a whale nor the spout of a whale that we knew of in all the time."

Many whalers later lamented the greed of those who destroyed their industry. One wrote of how he had once seen a whaler kill a female whale with her young in Delaware Bay to make a quick profit.

"Townsend's Inlet Bridge" (2019) Posted by Staib on Wikimedia Commons. Townsend's Inlet separates Sea Isle City to the north from Avalon on Seven Mile Beach to the south.

30.

Richard Somers replaces his father's log house on the hill with a brick "mansion."

John Somers died in 1723 at the age of 75. He and his wife Hannah had seven sons and three daughters. John Somers left his farm, with the log house on the hill, to his 30-year-old son, Richard.

In 1730, Richard replaced the log house with the two-story brick house that still stands in Somers Point. It has a small kitchen, dining, and living area on the first floor where the family gathered for meals. It has a master bedroom on the second floor where the parents slept, and a loft on the third floor where the children slept. However, for years, that modest brick house has been called "The Somers Mansion."

Richard Somers "burnt the brick" for his "mansion" in a nearby kiln. The pond in the middle of Somers Point today may have been where he and many others dug out the clay to make their bricks.

Two-story brick house built by Richard Somers in 1730 to replace his father's log house. It still stands in Somers Point and is known as "The Somers Mansion." Photo by Greg Sykora (2025)

Many West New Jersey settlers made bricks in their own kilns as soon as they arrived. In 1683, the Assembly in Burlington made a law requiring that all bricks sold be made a certain standard size. In 1698, Gabriel Thomas wrote that he saw "many fine, stately brick houses" in Philadelphia and in the West New Jersey towns of Salem and Burlington.

Most settlers who came from London built their homes with brick. They knew of the Great Fire of London of 1666. Settlers from other parts of England were more likely to build houses of wood.

"Pond in the Middle of Somers Point, New Jersey: 2025." Photo by Seth Grossman

Soon after Richard built his "mansion," Quaker meetings were held there instead of at the Meeting House. The Meeting House was then used as a school. Later, it was sold and used as a dwelling and blacksmith shop.

31.

James Somers builds a dam and two mills. He keeps his bargain in Bargaintown.

James Somers, Richard's younger brother, bought or inherited a "north field." It was a large tract of land north of Somers Point. Much of it is now in the town of Northfield, a suburb of Atlantic City.

Somers then built a dam across Patcong Creek to form a mill pond. He built and operated two mills powered by water flowing over that dam. One was a grist mill that ground corn into meal and wheat into flour. The other was a sawmill that cut logs into lumber.

According to a "persistent" local legend, James Somers bought several black slaves to help him build the dam. However, he made a "bargain" to free them when the work was done.

It is said that James Somers kept that bargain, set them free, and gave them plots of land to support themselves. That may explain why the area around that dam is still known as Bargaintown. Central Avenue runs over a new dam

Typical South Jersey dam and millpond at Batsto Vllage. A similar dam created the pond by Central Avenue between Linwood and Bargaintown. Another dam created the pond that once powered a mill by "Mill Road" in Absecon. New Jersey. Photo by Seth Grossman.

that is there today. It separates Northfield from Linwood, another Atlantic City suburb. It leads to Bargaintown Road in what is still Egg Harbor Township.

NOTE: No known documents support that "persistent" legend. However, the minutes of the April 29, 1799, meeting of the Gloucester County Society for the Abolition of Slavery in Woodbury do mention a "John Somers" of "Egg Harbor Township." They state that his heirs produced "papers confirming that he had previously freed one of his slaves before his death. She was a black woman named Jane Somers."

A typical gristmill stone used to crush corn and wheat kernels into meal and flour during the 1700s. On display near Shinn Log House in Mount Holly. Photo published by "MainstreetMountHolly.org."

James Somers may have also made bricks. There were large clay deposits in what is now Birch Grove Park in Northfield. Ponds were created when that clay was removed. There was a Somers Brick Company that mass-produced bricks in kilns near there from before 1900 until the 1930s. Its most popular brick was called the "New Jersey Red Colonial". The Somers family may have made bricks from that clay many years before then.

32.

Pennsylvania and West Jersey are "very great and inviting for poor people."

John Somers probably brought money with him when he arrived from England. He owned land in Pennsylvania before he bought land for his new farm in West New Jersey. His neighbors may also have brought money when they bought land around him.

However, in 1698, Gabriel Thomas wrote that West New Jersey and Pennsylvania were also "very great and inviting for poor people."

Thomas wrote that unskilled workers there were paid "three times the wages for their labor" than in "England or Wales." This included work as household servants in towns and as unskilled laborers on farms. He gave examples of skilled craftsmen earning far more and quickly becoming wealthy landowners.

Thomas also wrote that, besides earning more, people in Pennsylvania and West New Jersey paid less for food and lodging. He also said that people here "pay no tithes" and their taxes are "inconsiderable."

NOTE: Tithes were a 10% income tax used to support "established" churches. "Established" churches were supported and controlled by the government.

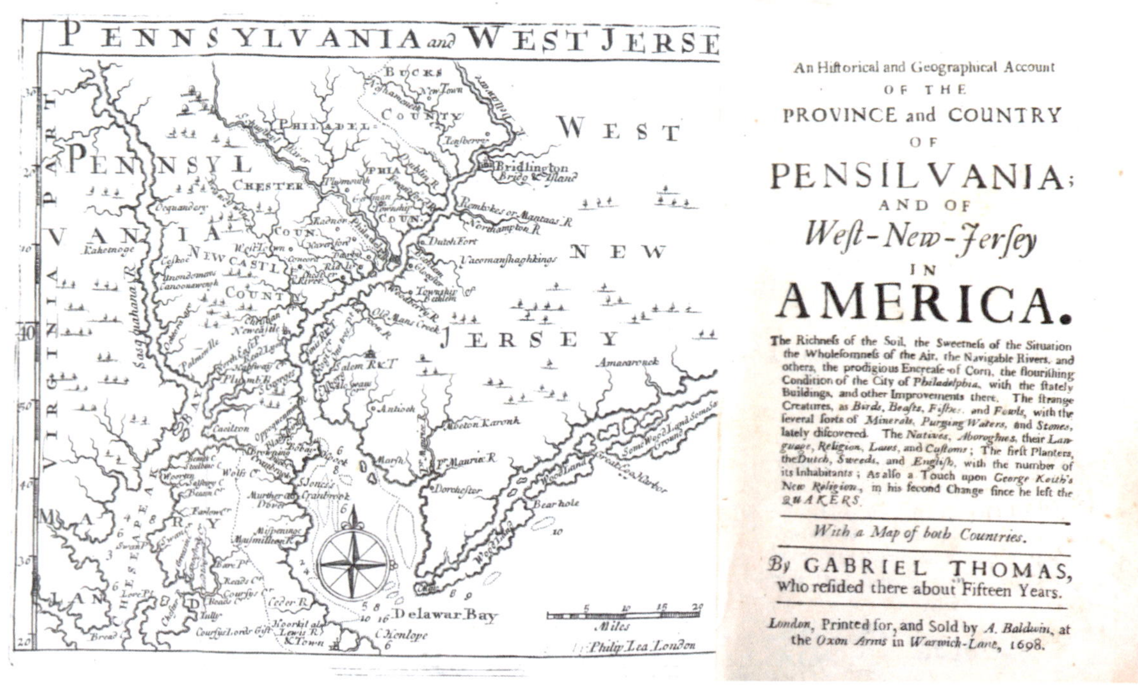

Cover Sheet and Map Insert of Pamphlet Published by Gabriel Thomas in London in 1698. From Internet Archive at archive.org. Public Domain.

Finally, Thomas reported that while vagabonds, beggars, and "poor laboring men. . . looking for employment they cannot find" were common sights in Britain, they were "nowhere to be seen" in Quaker-run Pennsylvania or West New Jersey.

Other West New Jersey settlers gave similar accounts. Mahlon Stacy from Burlington wrote this to his brother in England in 1680:

"I have seen this summer 40 bushels of bold wheat of one bushel sown… We have from May to Michaelmass (September 29) a great store of wild fruits, as strawberries, cranberries and hurtleberries. . . My brother Robert had as many cherries this year as would have loaded several carts. . . As for venison and fowls, we have great plenty. . . We caught herrings in the shallows of the river. . ."

Mahlon Stacy also wrote in 1680 that,

"I and eight others last winter bought a good ketch, freighted her out at our own charge and sent her to Barbados, and so to sail to "Saltertugas" (the British island of Tortuga near Venezuela that then produced salt.) to take in part of her lading in salt, and the rest in Barbados goods as she came back; which said voyage she hath accomplished very well". Smith, Samuel (1765). *The History of the Colony of Nova-Cæsaria, or New-Jersey, etc.* at pages 111-112.

FIG. 258. – KETCH.

A "ketch" is a two-masted sailboat with the shorter mast behind. Drawing by Georges Clerc-Rampal (1913). Published in "Freshwater and Marine Image Bank" by University of Washington (2016). Public Domain.

British historian Paul Johnson made a similar observation about all of Britain's North American colonies:

"Only 3 to 5 percent of middle-aged white males were poor. One-third of adult white males held no appreciable property, but these were under thirty. It was easy to acquire land. Over the course of a life-cycle, any male who survived to be forty could expect to live in a household of median income and capital wealth. In short, by 1775, America had a society that was predominantly middle-class. The shortage of labor meant artisans did not need to form guilds to protect jobs. It was rare to find restrictions on entry to any trade. Few skilled men remained hired employees beyond the age of twenty-five. If they did not acquire their own farm, they ran their own business. In practice, there were no real class barriers."

Paul Johnson, British Historian. (2010) PaulJohnsonArchives.org

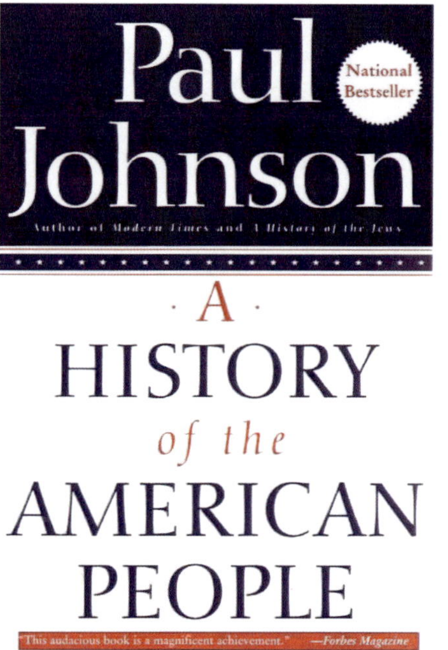

Johnson, Paul. (1997). A History of the American People. Harper Collins. Page 95

33.

Quakers buy and own black Africans as slaves in South Jersey and Pennsylvania

Quaker founder George Fox told his followers, "There is God in every man." That should have prevented them from buying, selling, or owning Africans, Native Americans, or anyone else as slaves. However, it did not. Many Quakers got rich by using black African slaves to grow and process tobacco and sugarcane in Barbados.

George Fox visited Barbados in 1671. He was clearly surprised and shocked by the brutal treatment of slaves that he saw there. He urged his followers to deal "mildly and gently" with their slaves and to free them "after thirty years' servitude." Later, Fox wrote that black slaves should freed after "a considerable term of years." He also instructed Quakers to worship together with slaves and to "train them in the fear of God."

Many Whites in Barbados angrily accused Fox and the Quakers of "teaching negroes to rebel." George Fox vigorously denied this. Fox did not do or say anything to oppose slavery there. He and other Quakers had very little power or influence in Barbados.

"English Quakers and Tobacco Planters in Barbados" (c1726), Illustration by Pieter van der Aa from Engraving by Carel Allard. Public Domain from Wikimedia Commons.

However, George Fox and William Penn did control West New Jersey and Pennsylvania. Yet neither said or did anything to stop Quakers from buying, selling or owning African slaves there. As a result, many Quakers did.

In 1690, William Penn reported that ten slave ships from the Caribbean had arrived in Philadelphia during the year.

In 1693, Gabriel Thomas boasted that Pennsylvania and West New Jersey were so prosperous that even his neighbor, a blacksmith, had a "Negro Man" to help him.

There was much work to be done and labor was scarce. Many Quakers claimed that they treated their African slaves as well as white indentured servants

Roughly one-half to two-thirds of European settlers to West New Jersey and Pennsylvania came as "Indentured Servants." About 75% were less than 25 years old. They made written contracts to serve their masters without pay for a fixed period of three to seven years. During this time, they received only food, lodging and clothing. They were subject to physical discipline and could not marry without the permission of their master.

European indentured servants willingly gave up their freedom. They did it to satisfy debts in Britain and pay for their two-to-three-month voyage to America. Most learned a useful trade or skill during their years of service. Most became financially independent and prosperous soon after their term of service ended.

Many Quakers claimed that they treated their black African slaves like white indentured servants. However, there were many obvious differences. African slaves did not willingly sell their freedom. Also, very few were set free after a "a considerable term of years." They and their children were usually sold as slaves when their owner died or could no longer use or afford them.

Some slaveowners claimed that the Bible permitted this. They relied on Genesis 4:8 to 4:15. That passage states "The LORD put a mark on Cain" after he killed his brother. They claimed that Blacks were descendants of Cain who deserved to be made slaves as punishment.

John Woolman and other opponents of slavery later responded to this by citing Genesis 7:1 to 7:10. This passage describes how only Noah and his family were saved by the Ark. The descendants of Cain, like everyone else, perished in the Great Flood.

Other slaveowners claimed that Blacks were descended from Canaan and relied on Genesis 9:25. This passage states, "Cursed be Canaan; He shall be the lowest of slaves to his brothers. . . Shem. . . (and) Japheth."

John Hepburn and other opponents of slavery later responded to this by saying that most Canaanites lived in the land of Canaan and were killed by Joshua when he conquered their land. Therefore, Black Africans were not the descendants of Canaan.

However, the most common argument made to justify slavery was that "the lives of negroes are so wretched in their own country, that many of them live better here than there."

Most slaveowners in West New Jersey claimed their slaves were treated kindly and made "part of the family."

However, both of those claims were challenged during a sensational criminal trial in Burlington in 1686. A well-known craftsman from a prominent Quaker family was indicted and put on trial for "giving blows" to a "Negro woman servant" that "occasioned her death."

34.

**A Burlington Quaker
is indicted for "giving blows"
to a "Negro servant woman"
that "occasioned her death."
A jury finds him "not guilty."**

James Wills was a "cooper" in Burlington. He was a skilled craftsman who made and repaired barrels. He was part of a prominent Quaker family, and his father was a respected doctor. James Wills owned several black slaves.

In 1686, a grand jury indicted him for "giving blows" to a "Negro woman servant" that "occasioned her death." He was also charged with burying her body without reporting her death to authorities. Wills pled not guilty.

The Governor of West New Jersey, together with six other justices, presided over his trial. The colony's attorney general prosecuted the case. He presented six witnesses.

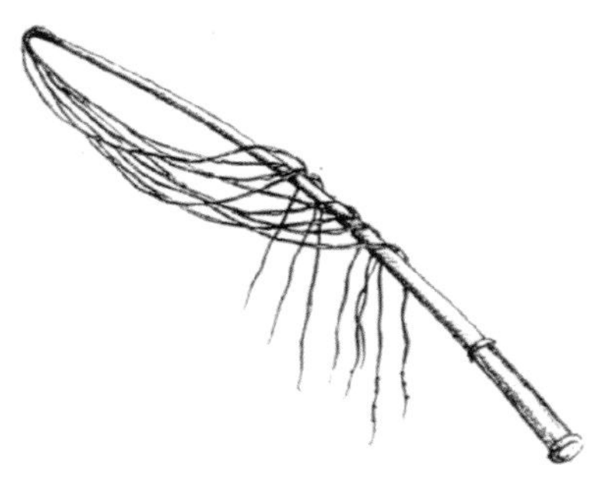

"'Cat-o-nine-tails' Whip" and "Slaver Flogging a Slave Woman Lashed to a Post" from "The House That Jeff Built" (1863) By David Claypoole Johnston. Although published during the American Civil War, some 200 years later, these images accurately depict how an eyewitness described the beating of a "Negro woman servant" in Burlington, West New Jersey, in 1686.

A husband and wife testified that Wills sent the "Negro woman" to their house so that their "Negro" could help her recover from "some distemper (illness)." They said the Negro woman's back was "very sore" from "fum fum" (beating). They said the Negro woman also had "a small scar upon her belly which was sore." The woman told them this was also from being beaten.

However, the couple then admitted, perhaps on cross-examination, that they "did not perceive any blows that in their judgment might be the cause of her death."

Another neighbor testified that while walking by, he "heard at a considerable distance many blows or stripes" and that he "heard the Negro cry out many times and so heard stripes or lashes continued until he got home." He said he "supposed it to be James Wills beating his Negro woman." He said he heard "still many lashes more and crying out" until he was "greeved." Then he said he "went into his house and shut the door." He testified that he then said to his wife, "Oh, yond cruel man." He estimated that he "heard full a hundred stripes or lashes."

However, he admitted that he "did not see James Wills beat his Negro."

A blacksmith and one of his workers testified that they were both working at a nearby shop. After hearing several stripes or lashes and one crying out, they "went forth." They then saw James Wills "beat his Negro servant and give her many stripes." This "greeved" them both. They then "went again to the shop to work."

A sixth witness testified that he saw James Wills "beat his Negro and tye her hands and hang her up." He said that her feet reached the ground and might sustain the weight of her body. However, he "believed it was painful to her" and that he "took her down."

That witness admitted, perhaps also on cross-examination, that "the Negro was so stubborn and willful that might well provoke any Master to use her sharply." He also admitted that he "saw nothing done to the Negro that in his judgment might be the cause of her death." He said he "believes" she was "unsound (unhealthy)."

After the trial, the jury "brought in this verdict:"

"We find the said James Wills not guilty. But in regard it appears the said Negro was unsound, it was a fault that he did not therefore be the more sparing. We also find Wills at fault to bury her without a Jury or Inquest."

As a result, Wills was ordered to pay all costs of his indictment and trial.

The death of this "Negro woman servant" clearly troubled many people in West New Jersey. Someone had to report the woman's disappearance. Someone had to demand and get an official investigation as to how she died. A grand jury of thirteen white men indicted a fellow Quaker. The Governor and six of the highest justices in the colony presided over the trial. The Attorney General of the province prosecuted the case.

However, the people of West New Jersey were not troubled enough to convict. Although three witnesses gave opinions that the injuries from the beatings were not severe enough to cause death, the jury was clearly "grieved" by the severe beating of a woman who was already ill.

Germantown Friends Petition against Slavery, 1688.

The Attorney General also failed to present the testimony of any of the Blacks who witnessed the incident. The name of the "Negro woman servant" was never mentioned in the court records.

Two years after the Burlington trial, Quakers of the Germantown Monthly Meeting near Philadelphia submitted a petition to the Yearly Meeting of all Quakers in Pennsylvania and West New Jersey. It urged them to "explain" why they permitted Christians to own Blacks as slaves. It read in part,

"How fearful and fainthearted are many on sea when they see a strange vessel. being afraid it should be a Turk, and they should be taken, and sold for slaves into Turkey. . . Is it worse for them which say they are Christians? For we hear that the most part of such Negroes are brought here against their will and consent, and that many of them are stolen. Now though they are black, we cannot conceive there is more liberty to have them slaves, as it is to have other white ones. There is a saying that we shall do to all men like as we will be done ourselves. . .

"And we who profess that it is unlawful to steal, must likewise avoid to purchase such things as are stolen, but rather help to stop this robbing and stealing if possible. . . Is Pennsylvania to have a good report? Instead it hath now a bad one for this sake in other Countries. Especially whereas the Europeans are desirous to know in what manner the Quakers do rule in their Province. Most of them do look upon us with an envious eye. But if this is done well, what shall we say is done evil?"

That Yearly Meeting of Quakers in Pennsylvania and West New Jersey took no action on this petition. It failed to respond in any way. The petition was discovered in the organization's archives 156 years later, in 1844.

35.

After thirty years, a few Quakers demand freedom for black slaves.

John Hepburn was a prosperous farmer who lived near Amboy in North Jersey. He came from Scotland in 1683 as an indentured servant working as a tailor.

In 1714, he published a 106-page book claiming it was "unlawful" for Christians to hold Blacks as slaves. Its full title was *The American Defence of the Christian Golden Rule: An Essay to Prove the Unlawfulness of Making Slaves of Men.*

Hepburn argued in detail that buying, selling, or owning Blacks as slaves violated the Golden Rule and each of the Ten Commandments. Hepburn refuted every argument he had heard to defend slavery. He called slavery a "vile contradiction of the Gospel of the Blessed Messiah." He warned of God's severe and unforgiving punishment of anyone who supported the enslavement of others in any way. That included buying sugar produced by slaves.

John Hepburn also begged for his own forgiveness for not acting sooner.

"I have lain dormant above this last thirty years for which I acknowledge my failure before God and Man. I desire the forgiveness of God, and next I desire the forgiveness of man. For the reason I was silent so long because I waited for my betters undertake the work. . ."

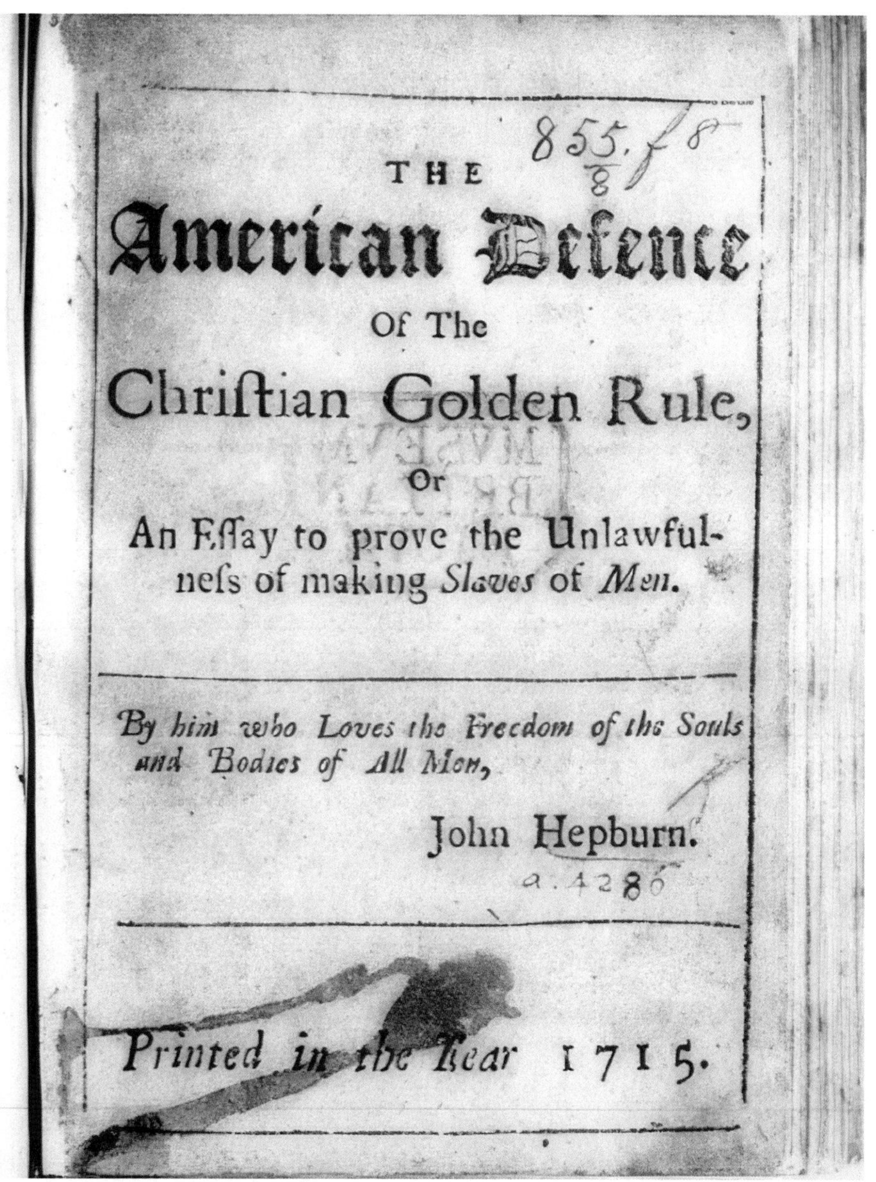

Front Page of Book Published by John Hepburn in 1715: "The American Defence of the Christian Golden Rule: An Essay to Prove the Unlawfulness of Making Slaves of Men."

Benjamin Lay was an English Quaker who had been a sailor. He moved to Philadelphia in 1732 when he was 50 years old. He immediately denounced the enslavement of Blacks there. He personally confronted and criticized Quakers who owned or traded in slaves. He attended as many Quaker meetings as he could to speak against them.

"Portrait of Benjamin Lay" (1750) by William Williams. Wikipedia. Public Domain.

In 1737, Lay published a book calling all Christians who owned or traded in slaves "apostates" and "sinners." He demanded that they be "disowned" and banned from Quaker meetings.

In 1738, Lay disrupted the yearly regional meeting of Quakers in Burlington, New Jersey. He took a container of red pokeberry juice and splashed it on the slaveowners he recognized there. He then shouted, "Thus shall God shed the blood of those persons who enslave their fellow creatures!"

Lay was immediately ejected from the meeting. He was then "disowned." He was barred from attending Quaker meetings in Pennsylvania and the southern part of New Jersey.[4]

ALL SLAVE-KEEPERS

That keep the Innocent in Bondage,

APOSTATES

Pretending to lay Claim to the Pure & Holy Chriſtian Religion ; of what Congregation ſo ever ; but eſpecially in their Miniſters, by whoſe example the filthy Leproſy and Apoſtacy is ſpread far and near ; it is a notorious Sin, which many of the true Friends of Chriſt, and his pure Truth, called *Quakers*, has been for many Years, and ſtill are concern'd to write and bear Teſtimony againſt ; as a Practice ſo groſs & hurtful to Religion, and deſtructive to Government, beyond what Words can ſet forth, or can be declared of by Men or Angels, and yet lived in by Miniſters and Magiſtrates in *America*.

The Leaders of the People cauſe them to Err.

Written for a General Service, by him that truly and ſincerely deſires the preſent and eternal Welfare and Happineſs of all Mankind, all the World over, of all Colours, and Nations, as his own Soul;

BENJAMIN LAY.

PHILADELPHIA:
Printed for the AUTHOR. 1737.

"Front Page of Book Published by Benjamin Lay in 1737". Its title is "All Slave-Keepers That Keep the Innocent in Bondage (are) Apostates."

---

4   NOTE: Both areas have been part of the same Quaker region since 1681. Between 1681 and 1760, Philadelphia and Burlington alternated as the site for the Yearly Meeting. After 1760, the Yearly Meeting for this Quaker region was always held in Philadelphia.

36.

A tailor from Mt. Holly shames Quakers into freeing their slaves.

During that time, a quiet young tailor from Burlington County, New Jersey, emerged. He succeeded where Hepburn and Lay had failed.

His name was John Woolman. During the next thirty years, he gently shamed Quakers in Pennsylvania and New Jersey into freeing their slaves.

Woolman was born in 1720 and raised as a Quaker. He worked on his father's farm in Rancocas, Burlington County, until he was 21. He then worked for a merchant in nearby Mount Holly.

When he was 23 years old, Woolman's employer asked him to prepare a bill of sale for a black slave woman he wanted to sell. This changed Woolman's life. Woolman later recalled,

"He was an elderly man, a member of our Society, and I wrote it. But after executing it, I was so afflicted in my mind, that I said before my master and the Friend that I believed slave-keeping to be inconsistent with the Christian religion."

From that moment on, Woolman worked tirelessly to end the owning and trading of slaves in England and America.

Woolman learned how to be a tailor. He constantly traveled between New Jersey and North Carolina, selling and fitting clothing. He attended and spoke at Quaker meetings wherever he went. He attended and spoke at churches where there were no Quaker meeting houses nearby. Woolman reached out to everyone he met in taverns, inns, and stagecoaches. Unlike Benjamin Lay, John Woolman was always gentle, patient, and respectful. He used relatable examples and parables. He was often described as "Christ-like."

John Woolman. Probably drawn from memory by his friend, Robert Smith, shortly after his death in 1772. Public Domain.

Woolman used almost every business, religious, and everyday conversation as an opportunity to persuade whoever he spoke to that slavery was an evil to be abolished. He urged every slaveowner he met to free his or her slaves at the earliest possible opportunity. He refused to draft wills for slaveowners unless they included a provision to free their slaves. He urged Quaker meetings and other church groups to adopt resolutions condemning slavery.

Woolman made Biblical arguments to those who relied on the Bible. He appealed to reason when speaking with those familiar with Enlightenment philosophers like John Locke.

Woolman said this when talking to an unnamed "thoughtful man", a "colonel in the militia" he met in Virginia.

"Men, having power, too often misapplied it. Although we made slaves of negroes, Turks made slaves of Christians. However, liberty is the right of all men equally."

After several years, John Woolman quit his business of selling and tailoring clothing. He became what Quakers call a "minister" or "elder." He spent all of his time teaching, writing, traveling, and speaking against slavery throughout America.

In 1754, Woolman wrote a pamphlet specifically instructing all Quakers to immediately free their slaves. It said that "All men by nature are equally entitled to the equity of the Golden Rule, and under indispensable obligations to it." This pamphlet was approved by the Quaker "Overseers of the Press" in Philadelphia and distributed at all Quaker meetings in the area.

In 1758, the Yearly Meeting for Quakers in Pennsylvania and the southern part of New Jersey recommended "without spoken dissent" that all Friends "set free those they hold in bondage." This was the same organization that expelled and "disowned" Benjamin Lay for demanding the same thing twenty years before.

That meeting also appointed John Woolman, Daniel Stanton, John Churchman, and other "ministers" and "elders" to a special committee. Their mission was to approach all slaveholding Quakers they encountered as they traveled. They were to remind them of their "Christian obligation" to free their "enslaved men, women, and children."

In 1772, John Woolman traveled to England. He urged Quakers there to help him end slavery throughout the British Empire. However, he soon became sick from smallpox and died there.

John Woolman kept a journal of his thoughts and experiences during his life. It was published shortly after his death as *The Journal of John Woolman*. It has been continuously published and sold ever since. It was recognized by John Stuart Mill and Charles Lamb as a great work of English literature and philosophy. It is in Volume 1 of the *Harvard Classics* collection.

In 1774, Quakers in Pennsylvania called for the "disownment" or shunning of Quakers who owned slaves. In 1775, they formed a Society for the Abolition of Slavery.

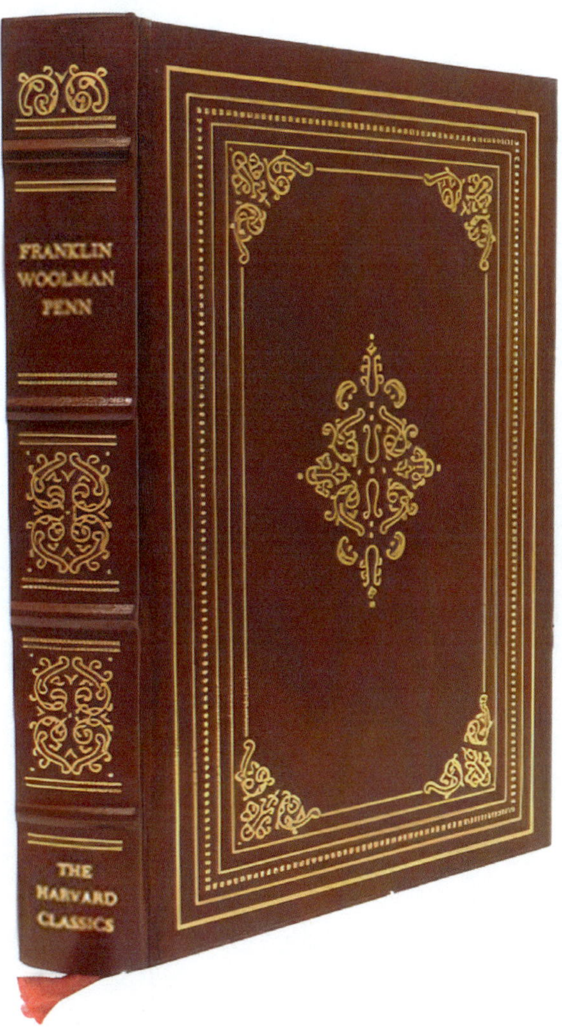

*Volume I of the **Harvard Classics**. It contains **The Autobiography of Benjamin Franklin**, the **Journal of John Woolman**, and **Fruits of Solitude** by William Penn. It is the first of 50 volumes containing hundreds of works chosen by Charles William Eliot, and first published in 1909. Eliot was the president of Harvard University from 1869 to 1909.*

37.

Ships are built, and iron is forged throughout South Jersey.

Mahlon Stacy was one of the first Quakers to settle in Burlington in 1678. One year later, he and *"eight others bought a good ketch, freighted her out at our own charge and sent her to Barbados."*

That small sailboat was almost certainly built nearby. British colonial records for the Port of Philadelphia show that ships built in South Jersey before 1776 had a total capacity of more than 4,000 tons. They included the 12-ton sloop *Speedwell,* built in Great Egg Harbor in 1730, and the 7-ton shallop *Endeavour,* built in Cape May in 1727.

Many ships built in South Jersey were not registered in Philadelphia. Some may have been registered at other ports. Many may not have been registered at all. Many Americans did that to avoid the taxes and restrictions of the British "Navigation Acts."

South Jersey was a perfect place to build wooden ships. It had abundant oak and cedar trees for lumber. It had pine trees to make tar and pitch. Many settlers were skilled carpenters and craftsmen who knew how to build them.

"Early Shipyard". Evans C. W. (1957), Virginia 350th Anniversary Celebration, Corp. Attribution Link: Evans, C. W., CC BY-SA 3.0 https://creativecommons. org/licenses/by-sa/3.0, via Wikimedia Commons

South Jersey had many deep-water rivers and creeks with easy access to the ocean. The Delaware River had deep water as far north as "the Falls" by Trenton. The Great Egg Harbor River had deep water as far as Mays Landing. It also had deep-water branches like Patcong Creek and English Creek. The Little Egg Harbor (Mullica) River had deep water as far as "The Forks." The Cohansey River had deep water as far as Bridgeton.

South Jersey also had iron. As early as 1675, blacksmiths noticed "bog ore" (limonite) in the mud of marshes and streams just south of what is now Red Bank in North Jersey. During the early 1700s, large amounts of bog ore were also found by Wading River, a branch of the Little Egg Harbor (now Mullica) River in Burlington County.

Iron rich "bog ore" (limonite) at site of former iron forge in Batsto, New Jersey in 2025. Photo by Seth Grossman

Cannonballs and a horseshoe made from bog ore on display at Batsto Village historical site near Hammonton, New Jersey. The cannonballs were produced later for the War of 1812. Photo by Seth Grossman

In 1715, a forge was built in Mount Holly to extract and refine that iron. During the next sixty years, other forges were built and operated in Lisbon, Trenton, Etna by Rancocas Creek, Batsto, and Atsion.

Those forges used bog iron to make iron nails and fittings for wooden ships. They also made tools and wrought iron rails. Later, during the War of 1812, they produced cannonballs.

Commercial production of bog iron in New Jersey ended in the 1840s. That was when abundant coal and iron deposits were found in nearby Pennsylvania.

Aetna Furnace, Tuckahoe River. Although built later, it was similar to the first furnaces to forge "bog iron" in Burlington County. Source: Heston, Alfred M., South Jersey a History 1664 to 1924 (Lewis Historical Publishing Co., 1924).

38.

New Jersey government is "extremely small, limited in its powers, and cheap."

In colonial New Jersey, the entire county government was often housed in two public buildings. One was a courthouse which also had offices for the clerk, surrogate, coroner, and tax assessor. The second was a nearby jailhouse where the sheriff had his office.

British Historian Paul Johnson wrote this description of New Jersey and the other British colonies in North America during the 1700s:

"They were the least taxed territories on earth. Indeed, it is probably true to say that colonial America was the least taxed country in recorded history.

"Government was extremely small, limited in its powers, and cheap. Often, it could be paid from court fines, revenue from loan offices, or sale of lands. New Jersey and Pennsylvania governments collected no statutory taxes at all for several decades.

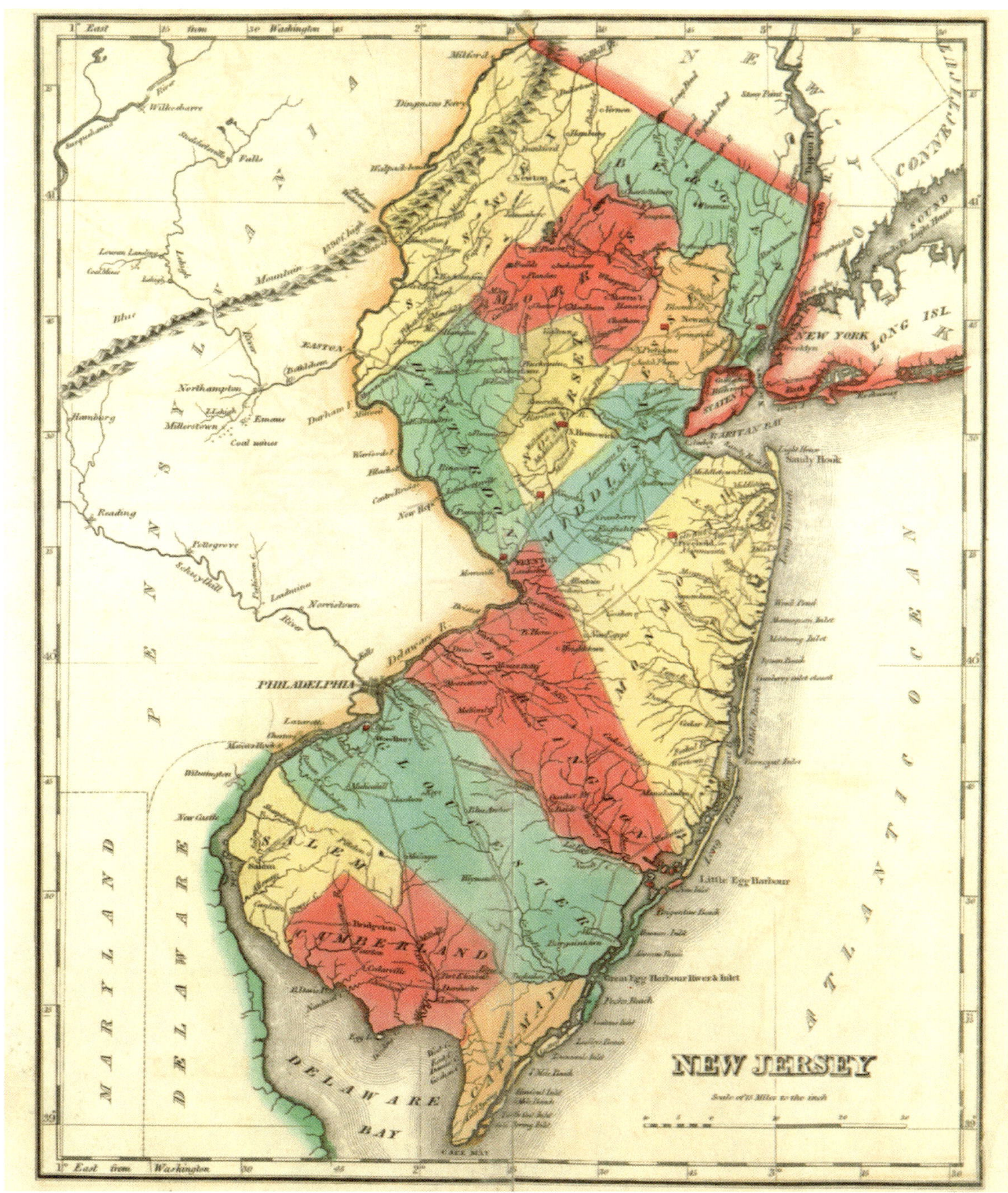

New Jersey had 13 Counties in 1822. Gloucester County with its Courthouse in Woodbury then included what are now Atlantic and Camden counties. Source: "Geographical, Statistical and Historical Map of New Jersey" from 1822 edition of Carey & Lea's Complete Historical, Chronological, and Geographical American Atlas, Philadelphia, Pennsylvania

"One reason why American living standards were so high was that people could dispose of virtually all their income. . . It was the closest the world has ever come to a no-tax society. . ."[5]

In 1692, the only tax imposed by the Assembly was a yearly head tax of 2 shillings and 6 pence for every person more than 16 years old. That would be roughly $31.40 per year today.

In 1693, the Assembly replaced the head tax with a property tax. The tax was one penny per year for one acre of improved land, 6 shillings for 100 acres of unimproved land, 6 pennies per year for each head of cattle or sheep and 12 pennies per year for a horse. In 1697, that tax rate was cut in half.

County governments also imposed taxes. In 1702, West New Jersey had four counties. They were Burlington, Gloucester, Salem and Cape May. Most of them had only a handful of paid officials. They usually included several judges and a Clerk, Sheriff, Surrogate, Coroner, and Tax Assessor.

Judges presided over civil and criminal cases. West New Jersey also had a unique informal court for small claims. This allowed litigants to quickly and inexpensively resolve small disputes without lawyers.

The Clerk kept and maintained a public record of every deed. This prevented disputes over land ownership.

The Sheriff enforced laws and judgments. He had the power to summon citizens to serve on juries. In unusual circumstances, he could summon men to bring arms and help him enforce the law. That power was called the "posse comitatus" or power of the community.

The Surrogate protected the rights of widows, orphans and others entitled to the property of those who died.

---

5   Johnson, Paul. (1997). *A History of the American People*. Harper Collins. Page 108

Most counties had a Coroner to investigate suspicious deaths. They also had a Tax Assessor to determine the value of real estate and farm animals that were taxed.

These county officials were usually paid with fees they collected from people who used their services.

Only landowners who lived in the county could vote. People who owned land were known as "freeholders." Each year they elected a "Board of Chosen Free-holders" for their county.

These Chosen Freeholders met from time to time to decide what roads, bridges, jails, and courthouses had to be built, maintained or repaired. They also decided how much money was needed to pay for them. That money was paid with a tax on real estate and farm animals.

NOTE: In 2020, the New Jersey Legislature and Governor Phil Murphy enacted a new state law saying that counties could no longer give those county officials the title of "Freeholder." Their title must now be "Commissioner". Lieutenant Governor Sheila Oliver said this was done because "People know the term is offensive and refers to a time when only white male landowners could hold public office."

(This is not true! Between 1776 and 1807, when voting laws were changed, all "inhabitants" of New Jersey "of full age" could and did vote and hold office if they were "worth 50 Pounds of Proclamation Money." This included Blacks and women.)

The Assembly divided most counties into smaller townships. Each township elected a "township committee" to build and maintain roads and bridges and provide other services not provided by the county. Township committees imposed additional taxes on real estate, buildings, and farm animals to pay for this.

Township committees also appointed constables to help county judges and the sheriff enforce the laws. Constables apparently received little

Women at the Polls in New Jersey in the Good Old Times" Engraving by Howard Pyle, Harper's Weekly. In 1880, this popular magazine published this image to remind its readers that women had voted in New Jersey between 1776 and 1807.

or no pay. Court records show that appointed constables often requested to be "excused" from their appointments. Some were held in contempt and punished for not accepting them. Some avoided constable duty by paying substitutes.

In 1693, the colonial government of West Jersey created Egg Harbor Township in Gloucester County. At first Egg Harbor Township included all of what is now Atlantic County. In 1774, it was split in half. The northern part became Galloway Township. At that time, it included what are now Hammonton, Mullica Township, Egg Harbor City, Port Republic, Brigantine, and Absecon.

Colonial voters, legislators, and county and township officials were usually thrifty. Only landowners paid real estate taxes. Only landowners who paid those taxes voted and held public office.

In 1703, Britain merged East and West New Jersey into one colony of New Jersey. However, the unified colony continued to have two capitals. The Assembly met in Perth Amboy for some sessions and in Burlington for others. The Governor resided in one town or the other.

39.

Few children go to public schools, but most learn "the three R's."

Properly educating children was very important to almost all Quakers and other Protestants in South Jersey.

They wanted their children to "fear the Lord" and do "His will on earth." Their children had to read and understand the Bible to do that. They also wanted their children to learn how to support themselves with honest, productive work and to manage their households.

These had been core beliefs of Protestants ever since Martin Luther publicly posted his 95 Theses in 1517. Martin Luther also translated the Bible from Hebrew, Greek and Latin into German in 1522 so everyone could read it. William Tyndale did it for English in 1525.

Each Christian parent, therefore, had a personal responsibility to teach reading, writing, and arithmetic (reckoning) to their children. Every Christian also had an obligation to make sure that orphans and children with parents too poor to do so were educated.

"Primitive New England School" Unknown Artist. Public Domain. This is what the first schools in West New Jersey also looked like.

In some South Jersey towns, boys were also expected to learn the basics of navigation at sea and of measuring and surveying land.

Well-off families hired tutors for their children. Others pooled their resources to hire teachers for the children of several families who lived near each other.

During this time, boys often became apprentices to learn skills from professionals, tradesmen, mechanics, or craftsmen. Masters of those skills were often required by law to also teach their apprentices what were later called "the three R's" (Reading, 'Riting and 'Rithmetic/Reckoning).

In 1685, Thomas Budd, a leading Quaker in Burlington, published a book called *Good Order Established in Pennsylvania and New Jersey.* In it, he recommended that the governments of both colonies provide public schools for children of parents who could not properly educate them.

Budd suggested that those parents "put their children seven years to the public school." There "persons of honesty, skill and understanding would be chosen… to teach boys and girls in all the most useful arts and sciences… as learning to read and write true English, Latin and other useful speeches and languages and fair writing, arithmetic and bookkeeping." Boys would also be "taught or instructed in some mystery or trade". Girls would also be taught "spinning of flax and wool, knitting of gloves and stockings, sewing, needle work and the making of strawwork."

To pay for these schools, Budd recommended that each city or town "give and lay out 1,000 acres in a good place" to "every public school that may be set up, and the rent or income of it go towards the defraying the charge of the school."

Caption: "Hornbook" used by children to learn basic reading, writing and arithmetic skills in America during the 1700s. Source: New York Public Library, Public Domain.

These schools would then be open to "children of poor people, and the children of Indians."

No such law was ever adopted by the Assembly of West New Jersey for the entire province. However, it did dedicate the 300 acres of Matinicunk (now Burlington) Island in the Delaware River to pay for public schools in the town of Burlington.

Also, many individual Quaker communities set up public schools to supplement private education. In 1722, Burlington allowed its meeting house to also be used as a school. Quakers in Egg Harbor Township in Gloucester County used their meeting house in Somers Point for a school after John Somers died in 1723.

Portrait of Benjamin Franklin painted by Joseph Duplessis in France in 1778. Source: National Portrait Gallery of the Smithsonian Institute via Wikimedia Commons.

It appears that most children in South Jersey got a basic education and that most adults were literate. In 1690, Michael Buffin asked the court in Burlington County to excuse him from being appointed constable because "he can neither read nor write". This indicates that literacy was an important qualification for even a minor position. It also shows that being illiterate was not common. The records of that court from 1680 to 1709 do not show any other instance of a constable being excused for that reason.

Although most children received a minimal, basic education from schooling, many later taught themselves more advanced subjects and skills.

Benjamin Franklin is a famous example. Although he grew up in Boston, Massachusetts, he was typical of many men and women in all of the colonies of British North America.

Franklin was the tenth of 17 children in his family. He had had two years of schooling that ended when he was ten years old. However, Franklin was an avid reader of books that he later bought, borrowed or shared. He formed groups and exchanged letters to discuss what he read. By doing this, Benjamin Franklin taught himself to become one of the most respected scientists, journalists, and political leaders in the world. Many other men and women in South Jersey and the rest of America did the same.

However, many Quakers were not satisfied with this basic education. In 1743, 23-year-old John Woolman taught briefly at the Quaker School in Mount Holly. There he worked with Anthony Benezet and others in Philadelphia to improve the quality of their "Friends Schools." They persuaded Quaker leaders to appoint qualified and dedicated trustees to professionally manage their schools. They recruited, trained, and hired talented, motivated teachers. They created new methods, books, and materials to inspire and engage students. They also taught students to care about the poor and disadvantaged in their communities.

Quakers in South Jersey and elsewhere made special efforts to educate those who did not have access to good schools. They opened special schools for girls. They enrolled orphans, the poor, Blacks, and Native Americans who could not pay tuition.

After these changes, "Friends Schools" in Philadelphia and South Jersey became respected for excellence in academics as well as teaching basic literacy and Quaker doctrines. Students were instructed in Latin, Greek, and French as well as in English. They were also taught of the need to avoid war and violence and to free all Blacks who were enslaved.

For years, the overnight Friends' boarding school in Burlington refused to en-roll girls. Its schoolmaster "thought it inconvenient to board a number of each sex in the same house."

However, in 1763, William Fentham, one of its teachers, arranged for his wife to instruct and board girls separately in a special "Girls Department." Girls boarded separately. They were "instructed in English, Writing, Arithmetic, and French" as well as "Needle-work." Quakers established a second school for girls in Burlington in 1778.

40.

Success and "the Golden Rule" make Quakers a minority in their own "homeland."

Many Quakers came to South Jersey and Pennsylvania because they were persecuted elsewhere.

Beginning in 1656, the Massachusetts Bay Colony* enacted a series of laws banning Quakers. Many Quakers defied that ban and were arrested. In 1658, Massachusetts Bay enacted a new law imposing the death penalty for any Quaker who openly preached in the colony after being expelled. Between 1659 and 1660, Massachusetts Bay executed four Quakers. One of them was Mary Dyer.

The Massachusetts Bay Colony was founded by Puritans in 1630. It was separate from the Plymouth Colony, run by "Separatists" known as the Pilgrims until 1691.

The Dutch also persecuted Quakers in Long Island when it was part of New Netherland. That persecution continued for years after Britain seized the colony in 1664.

"The Quaker Mary Dyer Led to Execution on Boston Common, June 1, 1660". (Around 1660, Unknown Artist, Brooklyn Museum. Source: Wikimedia Commons. Public Domain.

However, Quakers enjoyed spectacular success in South Jersey and Philadelphia, where they enjoyed equal rights.

"Philadelphia had been founded and shaped by Quakers. But the Quakers themselves had become rich. A tax-list of 1769 shows that they were only one in seven of the town's inhabitants, but that they made up half of those who paid over 100 British Pounds in taxes. Of the town's seventeen richest men, twelve were Quakers.

"Wherever the hard-working, intelligent Quakers went, they bred material prosperity which raised up others as well as themselves."[6]

By 1775, Philadelphia had roughly 40,000 people and was by far the largest city in British North America. At that time, the next largest cities were New York with roughly 21,000 people, Boston with 17,000, and Charleston, South Carolina with 12,000.

However, this success also attracted many non-Quakers from all over Europe and other American colonies. Quaker tolerance and commitment

---

6   *A History of the American People*, Paul Johnson, Harper Collins Publishers, New York (1997) Pages 108-109

to the "Golden Rule" gave all newcomers equal opportunities to succeed. By 1738, Quakers were a minority in both South Jersey and Philadelphia, their "Quaker Homeland."

A 1738 census showed that only 6,800 of the 17,150 people in Burlington, Gloucester, and Salem counties were Quakers. There were only 50 Quakers among the 1,200 inhabitants of Cape May County. Quakers were only 37% of the population of South Jersey.

"Morven". Richard Stockton's grandfather built the house on the left in Princeton in 1709. Richard Stockton, his grandson and signer of the Declaration of Independence added the addition on the right. Photo taken by Jack Boucher, 1964. Source: Library of Congress. Public Domain,

41.

Americans have a "Great Awakening" of Christian faith.

During the 1720s, many religious leaders in Britain and its American colonies warned that a dangerous decline in Christian worship, faith, and behavior was taking place.

Joseph Belcher, a prominent Christian historian, later described their concerns in his book *George Whitefield, a Biography*, published in 1857.

"The distinguishing doctrines of Christianity—the atonement, the work and office of Christ and the Spirit were comparatively lost sight of. The vast majority of sermons were miserable moral essays, utterly devoid of anything calculated to awaken, convert, save or sanctify…

"The highest personages in the land then lived openly in ways contrary to the law of God, and no man rebuked them. Profligacy (wasteful extravagance/moral looseness) and irreligion were reputable and respectable. Judging from the description we have of men and manners in those days, a gentleman might have

"George Whitefield Preaching in Bolton (England), June 1750." Painting By Thomas Walley, 1863. Source. Bolton Museum, U.K. Wikimedia Commons. Public Domain.

been defined as a creature who got drunk, gambled, swore, fought duels, and violated the Seventh Commandment (adultery), and for all this, very few thought the worse of him.

"Those too were the days when. . . (t)o be an infidel, to obtain power by intrigue, and to retain it by the grossest and most notorious bribery were considered no disqualification even for the highest offices. Such men indeed were not only tolerated, but praised."[7]

____

7   Belcher, Joseph, *George Whitefield, a Biography*, (American Tract Society, 1857) pp.16, 18 Posted online by Archive.org.

Although there was widespread wealth and comfort in America, hardship, death, and tragedy were never far away. Between 5% to 10% of all married women died in childbirth. Nearly half of all American children died before their fifth birthday. There was a spiritual need for faith, comfort, and purpose.

William Tennent was one of the first to call for a Christian revival. He was a Presbyterian minister who had previously lived and preached in Scotland and Ireland. In 1726, he moved to Neshaminy in Bucks County, Pennsylvania. Starting in the 1730s, he and his four sons preached in a new way that was personal and heartfelt. They traveled from town to town throughout New Jersey and Pennsylvania. They welcomed worshippers from all denominations and often spoke at large outdoor gatherings.

Tennent and his sons spoke of their own sins and shortcomings. They told of how they had overcome them by coming to Christ and beginning their lives anew. They invited others to do the same and share their hope and joy.

In 1727, William Tennent began teaching his methods to young preachers in a log house in Neshaminy. It became known as the "Log College." Its graduates travelled and preached throughout the British North American colonies.

George Whitefield grew up in Gloucester, England. He became an ordained minister of the Church of England in 1732, at age 18. However, he did not become a rector in a parish church. He instead traveled from town to town throughout England. He often preached to large outdoor crowds.

In 1738, George Whitefield sailed to Savannah, Georgia, to set up an orphanage. He then returned to America five more times during the next 30 years. Whitefield spoke at hundreds of small meetings and to many large outdoor crowds from Georgia to Massachusetts.

Whitefield often spoke of his own "conversion." He explained the spiritual experience that let him subdue and replace his "sinful passions" with "a complex habit of virtues."

However, he also shared personal experiences and made emotional connections with his listeners. When preaching to sailors near the docks of New York, Whitefield compared life to a sea voyage.

"Well, my boys, we have a cloudless sky and are making fine headway over a smooth sea before a light breeze and shall soon lose sight of land.

"But what means this sudden lowering of the heavens? And that dark cloud arising from beneath the western horizon? Hark! Don't you hear the distant thunder? Don't you see those flashes of lightning? There is a storm gathering! Every man to his duty! How the waves rush and dash against the ship! The air is dark. The tempest rages. Our masts are gone! What next?"[8]

"George Whitefield" (1742). Painting by John Wollaston. Source: National Portrait Gallery, London and Wikimedia.

One observer later wrote, "The unsuspecting tars, reminded of former perils of the deep, as if struck by the power of magic, arose and with united voices exclaimed, "Take to the longboat, sir!"

"You can well imagine how this natural answer would be used by the preacher."

8 Belcher, Joseph, *George Whitefield, a Biography*, (American Tract Society, 1857) pp.16, 18 Posted online by Archive.org.

42.

George Whitefield awakens Philadelphia and South Jersey.

In 1739, George Whitefield came to Philadelphia. He spoke from the balcony of the Old Courthouse at Second and Market Streets. Benjamin Franklin, a religious skeptic, went as a scientist to observe him and his audience.

Franklin carefully walked through and around the crowd. He carefully listened to what Whitefield was saying and how people responded to him. Franklin estimated that out of a much larger crowd, at least 25,000 to 30,000 people could clearly hear "every word." At the end of the sermon, Franklin wrote that he and an equally skeptical friend were so impressed that they "emptied their pockets of all coins, including the gold" and put them "in Whitefield's collection dish."

Benjamin Franklin later published Whitefield's sermons and delivered them throughout America.

Whitefield spoke to all Christians. He ridiculed the differences that often divided them. Once, when speaking in Philadelphia, Whitefield openly imagined having this conversation with the Old Testament Patriarch Abraham:

"Father Abraham, who have you in heaven? Episcopalians?" "No". "Any Presbyterians?" "No." "Any Baptists?" "No." "Have you any Methodists, Seceders or Independents?" "No. No. No!"

"Why who have you there?" "We don't know those names here. All who are here are Christians—Believers in Christ—Men who have overcome by the blood of the Lamb and the word of his Testimony?"

"Oh is that the case? Then God help me. God help us all to forget the party names and to become Christians in deed and truth!"

Whitefield even recalled attending services at a Jewish synagogue in Gibraltar. He said he went there when his ship from England stopped there on its

"The Old Courthouse, Philadelphia (1789)", Unknown Artist, 1876 Commonwealth Pennsylvania History Illustrated, posted by Wikimedia Commons, Public Domain.

"Deerfield Presbyterian Church" Built in 1771. In 1732, a new Presbyterian con-gregation there built a log schoolhouse. In 1737, it built a new "meeting house". In 1767, the congregation began gathering stones and building this meeting house. It was completed in 1771. It is still in use today. Photo by unknown photographer made before 1923. Source: Presbyterian Historical Society. Posted on Wikimedia Commons. Public Domain.

way to Georgia. Whitefield said the rabbi invited him to sit at the "chief seat." The rabbi said he had heard Whitefield preaching against "profane swearing" the day before and wanted to thank him.

During 1740 and again in 1746, George Whitefield spoke throughout South Jersey. He attracted and energized large crowds at outdoor meetings in Gloucester, Greenwich in Cohansey, Salem, Cape May, Cedar Bridge (Bargaintown), Burlington and Maidenhead (now Lawrence Township). He also preached to young Native American men at their settlement in Brotherton (now Indian Mills).

During those years, Jonathan Edwards a Puritan from Connecticut, Jonathan Dickinson, a Presbyterian from Massachusetts, and the four sons of William Tennent, also gave emotional, inspiring sermons to large outdoor crowds. Jonathan Edwards reached thousands more by publishing his sermons.

All of this made Bible values, Christian faith, and church attendance an important part of everyday American life again. This Christian revival became known as "The Great Awakening."

The Great Awakening inspired the formation and expansion of many new congregations and the building of many new churches throughout South Jersey.

They included new Presbyterian churches in Pilesgrove (Pittsgrove), Deerfield, Fairfield, Timber Creek (Blackwood) and Cold Spring, and the Forks of Little Egg Harbor (Pleasant Mills). They also included Baptist churches at Mill Hollow near Salem, Daretown, and Dividing Creek.

The Great Awakening encouraged congregations of different denominations to share buildings, chairs, and benches, and to attend each other's events.

In 1761, Andrew Blackman donated land to build a new "Presbyterian Meeting House" on Zion Road in the area of Egg Harbor Township known as "Cedar Bridge" (Bargaintown). The deed specified that the building be available for "public religious worship for all that shall incline to meet and assemble in it." Methodists began using it in 1789. Today it is the Zion Methodist Church. Enoch "Nucky" Johnson, who dominated Atlantic City politics from 1913 to 1941, is buried in its cemetery.

In 1746, Jonathan Dickinson co-founded the College of New Jersey together with graduates of the "Log College" of William Tennent. He also served as its first President. In 1754, George Whitefield gave the commencement address and received an honorary "Master of Arts" degree.

In 1758, Jonathan Edwards became its third President. The College of New Jersey later became Princeton University.

While Whitefield and the others were preaching in America, John Wesley was leading a similar evangelical movement in England. It was later called "Methodism." In 1771, Wesley sent 26-year-old Francis Asbury to preach his doctrine and establish Methodist Churches throughout America. He did that for the next forty years.

Asbury established many new Methodist churches in the Quaker-settled counties of South Jersey including these:

Absecon Methodist Church in 1796, Head of the River Methodist Church in Estell Manor in 1792, Olivet Methodist Church in Centerton in 1773, the Friendship Methodist Church in Salem and Trinity Methodist Church in Pennsville in 1775, Port Elizabeth Methodist Church in 1778.

Asbury's fierce opposition to slavery appealed to many Quakers. Asbury later suggested that America's War for Independence was a just cause that good Christians could fight for. This appealed to many younger Quakers.

43.

Quakers are also awakened, and free more slaves.

The Great Awakening also inspired Quakers. Quakers emphasized equality at their worship meetings. However, they recognized that some members had special talents to instruct and inspire others. They were called "elders" or "ministers." They were encouraged to travel and speak to many different meetings.

During the Great Awakening a new generation of Quaker elders and ministers emerged. They also gave personal, heartfelt sermons that inspired and energized those who heard them. They also traveled and attracted crowds throughout South Jersey and other colonies. They especially appealed to young people.

They were also popular with Christians in other denominations. They often spoke in churches when Quaker meeting houses were too small or far away. Members of other churches often went to hear Quaker preachers who came to their towns. They often loaned Quakers their benches and chairs.

Daniel Stanton, John Griffith, Isaac Andrews, and John Churchman were among the best-known Quakers who preached in South Jersey. Ironically, John Woolman rarely spoke there even though he lived in Mount Holly..

"Trinity African American Episcopal Church of Gouldtown, NJ". The congregation was formed in 1818. It purchased an old schoolhouse for worship in 1823. Although this church was not built until 1860, its congregation was formed in 1818. Gouldtown was settled as an integrated, mixed-race community that included free, land-owning African Americans and Native Americans as well as Whites. Photo taken in 2010 by Smallbones and released into the Public Domain. Posted online by Wikimedia Commons.

Some of the most effective and best-known Quaker elders and ministers were women. They included Elizabeth Smith, Hannah Foster, and Ann Gaunt. Ann Gaunt grew up in Tuckerton. As a young girl, she began preaching the gospel at the Quaker meeting house at Little Egg Harbor. She later routinely spoke at Quaker meetings as far away as Massachusetts.

Quaker elders and ministers often differed from other traveling preachers by emphasizing deeds over words and feelings. They spoke of the need to do God's work on earth. They constantly spoke of the urgent need to free black slaves.

During this time, Joshua Evan, a Quaker elder from Gloucester County told his followers not to buy or use sugar, cotton, or any products made with slave labor.

The Great Awakening allowed Quakers to deliver that message to far more people than ever before.

In 1777, the Quaker Annual Meeting in Burlington appointed two members "to call upon members of the Woodbury and Haddonfield meetings who continued to hold slaves." As a result, more than 15 slaves were freed. In that same year, a "manumission committee" of the Quaker Meeting of Salem reported that it had persuaded Quakers there to free more than 30 slaves.

In 1780, the Pennsylvania Legislature passed laws to gradually end slavery there.

Quakers in New Jersey formed a Society for the Abolition of Slavery in 1786. However, most Blacks in the Quaker majority counties of Burlington, Gloucester, and Salem were already free.

At its meeting of September 2, 1796, the "Gloucester County Society for the Abolition of Slavery" reported that at least 350 Blacks were living there. Of them, 29 were slaves, and the other 321 were free. The Society instructed its members to locate all Blacks in the county so they could take action to free those who were still slaves. They also brought lawsuits to free any Blacks, especially children, who they believed were illegally held as slaves. The Society also raised funds and found teachers to educate all black children.

Some Quakers granted tracts of land to their freed slaves so they could support themselves.

At its meeting in Woodbury on April 29, 1799, the Gloucester County Society found 462 Blacks living in Gloucester County. Of them, 47 were slaves and 415 were free. It found that of the free Blacks, 92 were "householders", "freeholders" or "mechanics" who were qualified to vote at that time.

That was the same meeting where the Clerk received papers confirming that John Somers of Egg Harbor Township had freed one of his slaves before his death.

During this time, there were several communities of free Blacks in West New Jersey. The oldest was Gouldtown near what is now Bridgeton. Gouldtown is today part of Fairfield Township in Cumberland County. It was formed when Elizabeth Adams, the granddaughter of John Fenwick married a free black man named Gould against his wishes. John Fenwick was one of the original proprietors of West NewJersey. At one time, he owned one-tenth of all land in the colony. He led the first Quakers to Salem in 1675.

Copy of Manumission Record of Peter Hill Recorded with Clerk of Burlington County, New Jersey in 1794. From Wikimedia Commons. Public Domain. It states: "To all whom it may concern, I do hereby for myself & my heirs manumit and set free my Negro or Mulatto Man Peter Hill, aged 27 years on July 19, 1794

Free Haven, now known as Lawnside, was another thriving community of free Blacks. Although now within Camden County, Lawnside was then part of Gloucester County. Free Blacks began to settle there during the late 1700s.

44.

South Jersey becomes part of a new American nation.

According to British historian Paul Johnson:

"The 'Great Awakening' was. . . the formative moment in American history that preceded the political drive for independence and made it possible. It crossed all religious and sectarian boundaries and made light of them. It turned what had been a series of European-style churches into American ones."

"It began the process which created an ecumenical and American type of religious devotion which affected all groups and gave a distinctive American flavor to a wide range of denominations. This might be summed up under the following five heads:

> *1. Evangelical vigor.*
> *2. A tendency to downgrade the clergy*
> *3. Little stress on liturgical correctness*
> *4. Even less stress on parish boundaries.*
> *5. An emphasis on individual experience."*

"Its key text was Revelations 21:5: 'Behold, I make all things new'—which was also the text for the American experience as a whole. . ."

"The Great Awakening also taught the different colonies. . . to grasp and appreciate what they had in common, which was a very great deal. As a symbol of this, Whitefield was the first 'American' public figure. He was equally well known from Georgia to New Hampshire. When he died in 1770, there was comment from the entire American press."[9]

Not all Americans approved of this "Great Awakening". Many rejected appeals to emotion. Many objected to preachers who traveled rather than minister to their own congregations. Several congregations in South Jersey divided into different factions with names like "Old Side" and "New Side", "Old School" and "New School," or "Old Light" and "New Light."

Even those who openly supported the Great Awakening sometimes privately expressed doubts. John Woolman worried that "inspired pulpit oratory" could "prevent the faithful from searching for and finding their own Inner Light."

Woolman also wanted Christians to "live in the spirit of truth." He wanted them to be judged by their "fruits," not words. Woolman taught the importance of freeing slaves, avoiding wars, and helping the poor. He often quoted scripture and emphasized the importance of reading and learning.

Woolman warned against neglecting "duty as members of a family or civil society" by spending too much money on "too liberal use of spiritous liquors" and "the custom of wearing too costly apparel." Quaker John Churchman emphasized the need for "inspiration" before speaking and "doers" instead of "words."

These different views were often published in letters, pamphlets, and newspapers throughout the British colonies of North America.

---

9   Johnson, Paul. (1997). *A History of the American People.* Harper Collins. Page 116

The Seal of the State of New Jersey Adopted by Its Legislature in 1777. It depicts the Roman Goddess of Liberty on the Left and the Roman Goddess Ceres (or Abundantia), representing prosperity, on the Right. Liberty holds a wooden pike, draped with a red Phrygian cap. The goddess for Prosperity holds a cornucopia. The pike was the traditional weapon of ordinary citizens. It was only effective when every citizen turned out to use it. According to legend, the red cap was worn in Roman times by slaves who had gained their freedom. The Cornucopia (Horn of Plenty) was a Roman symbol of prosperity.

Religious differences often became political. That is because nine British colonies in America had "established" churches funded by taxes. The Church of England was "established" in New York, Maryland, Virginia, North and South Carolina and Georgia. The Congregational Church was established in Massachusetts, Connecticut and New Hampshire.

Religious differences became political when people resented paying taxes for churches they did not attend and doctrines they did not support. This grew worse during the Great Awakening when attendance at established older churches declined, while new congregations struggled to raise funds to build their churches.

This was not a problem in New Jersey, Pennsylvania, Delaware or Rhode Island. The three Quaker-settled colonies plus Rhode Island had no established churches or taxes or tithes to pay for them. Private donations paid for all of the new churches built there during the Great Awakening. They also paid the salaries of their clergy.

When all congregations raised their own funds privately, they did not compete against each other for government funding. They often helped each other and attended each other's events.

This was the beginning of a new American idea that became a fundamental part of American culture many years later. Americans learned that there was less hatred and violence over religion when political leaders did not fund any churches or take sides in any religious disputes.

"Liberty and Prosperity" had not yet become the motto of New Jersey. However, the national exchange of ideas during this "Great Awakening" helped Quakers and others in South Jersey and Philadelphia see themselves as part of a larger American nation with an abundance of both. It made the rest of America aware of the values and ideas that brought success to the "Quaker Homeland" that became South Jersey.

South Jersey
(and rest of the world) timeline

1453: Muslim Ottoman Turks seize Christian Constantinople and control the Mediterranean Sea.

1492: Christopher Columbus leaves Italy and crosses the Atlantic Ocean for Spain. He claims "The West Indies" for Spain.

1498: John Cabot (Giovanni Caboto) leaves Italy and crosses the Atlantic Ocean for England. He claims most of North America (including what is now New Jersey) for England.

1517: Martin Luther teaches Christians in Germany to be guided by the Bible instead of priests.

1524: Giovanni da Verrazano leaves Italy and crosses the Atlantic for France.

1529: Pope Leo X condemns Martin Luther as a "heretic." Charles V of Spain goes to war against "Protestants" who "protest."

1534: King Henry VIII takes the churches of England away from the Pope. However, he persecutes and executes Protestants who want a "Reformation".

1558: Elizabeth I becomes Queen and makes England safe for Protestants.

1560: Spain and Italian states form a "Holy League" to fight the Ottoman Turks on land and sea.

1588: Spanish Armada fails to subdue England.

1600s:	The Church of England persecutes "Separatists" and "Dissenters."
1607:	England "plants" settlers in Jamestown, Virginia.
1614:	Dutch merchant and ship captain Cornelius Jacobson Mey visits and names Cape May and Egg Harbor.
1619:	Dutch privateers sell 20 African slaves to English settlers in Jamestown, Virginia.
1620:	England tolerates "Separatists" if they move to America. The "Pilgrims" settle in Massachusetts.
1623:	The Pilgrims feast and give thanks when they end "community" ownership of land.
1624:	The Dutch establish "New Netherland" along the Hudson River and on Long Island.
1638:	Swedes and Finns settle in "New Sweden" by the Delaware River.
1642 through 1651:	England is divided and weakened by civil wars.
1647:	George Fox starts the Quaker movement in England.
1655:	The Dutch seize New Sweden and settle along the Delaware River.
1660:	Parliament unites England. Charles II becomes King, and his brother James, Duke of York, becomes "Lord Admiral" of the Royal Navy.
1661:	King Charles II proclaims that Quaker meetings are "unlawful."
1664:	(February) Carteret and Berkeley sign "Concessions and Agreements" as a constitution for New Jersey while the Dutch still own it.

1664:	(March) King Charles gives all of "New England" (which includes Dutch "New Netherland") to his brother James, Duke of York.
1664:	(May): Captain Richard Nicolls leaves England with four warships to capture New Netherlands.
1664:	(June) James gives New Jersey to George Carteret and John Berkeley.
1664:	(October) The Dutch surrender New Netherland to the British without a fight.
1670:	There are roughly 50,000 Quakers in England. Some 1,300 are in prison. William Penn is arrested and put on trial for preaching to a crowd in the street.
1672:	George Fox explores New Jersey
1673:	George Fox and William Penn make plans for a "Quaker Homeland" in New Jersey.
1674:	Quakers buy half of New Jersey from John Berkeley.
1675:	John Fenwick establishes Salem as the first Quaker settlement in West Jersey.
1676:	Quakers and George Carteret divide New Jersey into "East" and "West."
1676:	West Jersey Quakers adopt a new "Concessions and Agreements" written by William Penn and Edward Byllynge.
1677:	Quakers settle in Burlington.
1677:	Quakers bargain and pay for land claimed by Native Americans.

1680:	James, Duke of York, recognizes and approves Quaker rights to govern West Jersey.
1681:	First elected West Jersey Assembly meets in Burlington.
1680s:	John Somers builds a "log house" by the "point" between the river and the Great Egg Harbor.
1680s:	Somers and his neighbors live prosperous, comfortable lives.
1685:	West New Jersey Assembly dedicates a 300-acre island in the Delaware River to fund public schools in Burlington.
1686:	Slaveowner in Burlington acquitted after trial for "occasioning" the death of a "Negro woman servant."
1690:	Ten ships with African slaves from the Caribbean arrive in Philadelphia.
1692-1694:	West Jersey creates counties and county governments for Burlington, Cape May, Gloucester, and Salem. (Gloucester includes what are now Atlantic and Camden.)
1702:	East and West New Jersey again become one British colony of New Jersey.
1714:	John Hepburn publishes book denouncing slavery as "anti-Christian."
1715:	Bog iron is forged at Mount Holly.
1738:	Census confirms that Quakers are a minority in their West Jersey "homeland."
1739:	George Whitefield brings the "Great Awakening" to Philadelphia and South Jersey

1743:	John Woolman of Mount Holly shames most Quakers into freeing their slaves.
1748:	Assembly creates Cumberland County out of Salem County.
1756:	Bands of Lenni Lenape attack and kill settlers near the Delaware Water Gap.
1758:	Lenni Lenape sign the "Treaty of Easton". Most leave New Jersey for payment of $1,000 Spanish dollars and promise of land near Ohio River.
1758:	Quaker Yearly Meeting for Philadelphia and Burlington "recommends" that Quakers free their slaves.
1796:	Gloucester County, New Jersey has 321 free Blacks and 29 slaves.

About the Author

Seth Grossman is a lifelong resident of Atlantic City, New Jersey, with a passion for its local history. He is a graduate of Duke University and Temple Law School. He has been a practicing attorney in and around Atlantic City since 1975. Between 2010 and 2017, he was an adjunct professor of U.S. History at Atlantic Cape Community College. He has been the Executive Director of Liberty and Prosperity 1776, Inc. since its founding in 2003. He is a regular guest on several popular talk radio programs heard in and around South Jersey and Philadelphia.

Author Seth Grossman on the Atlantic City Boardwalk.
(Photograph by Vernon Ogrodnek)

Liberty and Prosperity 1776, Inc. was established as a tax-exempt educational charity in New Jersey in 2003. Its mission is to teach why "Liberty and Prosperity", New Jersey's motto since 1777, is true and relevant today and how Americans can again become free and effective citizens. Its website is **LibertyAndProsperity.com**

Sources, Credits, and Suggestions for Further Reading

1.   AN ICE AGE CREATES A LAND BRIDGE FROM ASIA. NATIVE AMERICANS MIGRATE TO AMERICA.

a.   Freson Michelle, "The Chumash: The Seashell First People Of North America", Ancient-Origins.net on October 12, 2021

b.   Geggel, Laura, "The 1st Americans Were Not Who We Thought They Were", Live Science.com, October 9, 2023, https://www.livescience.com/archeology/the-1st-americans-were-not-who-we-thought-they-were

c.   Winter, Dr. Barbara, "A Journey to a New Land", sfu.museum.virtualmuseum.ca, Archived from the original on 28 April 2015, Retrieved 19 May 2015. Simon Frasure Museum of Archeology and Ethnology. http://www.sfu.museum/journey/an-en/

d.   Yukon Beringia Interpretive Centre, "The First People", October 29, 2025. https://beringia.com/exhibits/first-people

2.   ALGONQUIANS AND IROQUOIS MOVE NORTHEAST AS THE EARTH WARMS.

a.   Harriott, Thomas. "A Briefe and True Report of the New Found Land of Virginia" (1588). Part 3. Posted online by U.S. National Park Service at https://nps.gov/fora/learn/education/the-third-and-last-part.htm

b.   Julian, Charles. "A History of the Iroquoian Languages" (2010). University of Manitoba. https://mspace.lib.umanitoba.ca/server/api/core/bitstreams/6b2df4a6-c15a-4d2d-8042-a189bf638df4/content

c.   Lake Hopatcong Historical Museum. "Historical Perspective of Lake Hopatcong" (2025). http://lakehopatcong.org/history%20of%20Lake%20Hopatcong.htm

d.   SeaGrant,University of Wisconsin, "The Formation of the Great Lakes-How They Were Made" (2025). https://www.seagrant.wisc.edu/resources/the-formation-of-the-great-lakes/how-they-were-made/

e.   Thomas, Gabriel. *Historical and Geographical Account of Pennsylvania and West New Jersey.* (A Baldwin, 1698). pp. 13, 66-67 https://www.si.edu/object/account-pennsylvania-and-west-new-jersey-gabriel-thomas-reprinted-original-edition-1698-introduction:siris_sil_1106641

3. LENNI LENAPE SPEAKERS ROAM IN AND AROUND WHAT IS NOW SOUTH JERSEY.

a. DiCostanzo, David A. "History of the Lenni Lenape Before, During, and After the American Revolution", *NJ Council for Social Studies.* January 13, 2023 (2023). https://teachingsocialstudies.org/2023/01/13/lenni-lenape-before-during-and-after-the-american-revolution/

b. Elmer, Lucius Q.C., *History of the Early Settlement and Progress of Cumberland County* (1869). West Jersey History Project. (2025) https://westjerseyhistory.org/books/Elmer/

c. Foley, Gerard, "The Esopus Wars: Dutch Aggression against Lenape Natives", *The Hudson River Valley Review.* (2025) https://www.hudsonrivervalley.org/documents/d/guest/esopus_wars_foley

d. Goodspeed, Marfy, "By Their Names You Shall Know Them" (2/17/13), *Goodspeed Histories: New Jersey History and Genealogy*, https://goodspeedhistories.com/by-their-names-you-shall-know-them/

e. Historical Society of West Windsor, "Indigenous Peoples" (2025). *West Windsor History Book.* https://www.westwindsorhistory.com/book.html

f. Krykew, Sara. "A Short History of the Lenni Lenape" (2016). *Chadds Ford Historical Society.* https://chaddsfordhistorical.wordpress.com/2016/06/26/a-short-history-of-the-lenni-lenape/

g. Licht, Loyd, Duffin, & McConaghy. "The Original People and Their Land: The Lenape, Pre-History to the 18th Century". (2009) *West Philadelphia Collaborative History. University of Pennsylvania.* https://collaborativehistory.gse.upenn.edu/stories/original-people-and-their-land-lenape-pre-history-18th-century

h. McCarthy, Jack (Project Director). "The Original People: The Lenape on the Poquessing" (2025). *Preservation Alliance for Greater Philadelphia.* https://preservationalliance.com/the-original-people-the-lenape-on-the-poquessing/

i. Norwood, John R., "We Are Still Here!", (2007*). Native New Jersey Publications.* https://www.nanticoke-lenape.info/images/We_Are_Still_Here_Nanticoke_and_Lenape_History_Booklet_pre-release_v2.pdf

j. Rementer, James. "Arrival of the Europeans As Told by the Lenape". (2025). *Delaware Tribe.org.* https://delawaretribe.org/wp-content/uploads/Arrival-of-the-Europeans.pdf

k. Smith, Samuel (1765). *The History of the Colony of Nova-Cæsaria, or New-Jersey, etc. (WS Sharp, 1877) pp 22-25* https://archive.org/details/bim_eighteenth-century_the-history-of-the-colon_smith-samuel_1765

l. Thomas, Gabriel, *supra,* at p. 13

m. Thomas, Pegg. "Lenni Lenape and their Wars" (2019). *Colonial Quills.* https://colonialquills.blogspot.com/2019/05/lenni-lenape-and-their-wars.html

4. **MANY LENNI LENAPE NEAR THE DELAWARE RIVER SPEND SUMMERS BY THE SOUTH JERSEY SHORE.**

a. Atlantic County Government, *"Lenni Lenape: Native Americans of New Jersey"* (2025). Atlantic County Government https://www.atlanticcountynj.gov/government/government-information/history-of-atlantic-county/lenni-lenape-native-americans

5. **A TURKISH "GHAZI" IN THE MIDDLE EAST STARTS EVENTS THAT BRING EUROPEANS TO AMERICA.**

a. Cartwright, Mark. "Trade in the Byzantine Empire" (2018) . *World History Encyclopedia.* https://www.worldhistory.org/article/1179/trade-in-the-byzantine-empire/

b. Cartwright, Mark. "Trade in Medieval Europe" (2019). *World History Encyclopedia.* https://www.worldhistory.org/article/1301/trade-in-medieval-europe/

c. Encyclopedia Britannica. "Ottoman Empire – Osman, Orhan, Expansion" (2025). https://www.britannica.com/place/Ottoman-Empire/Osman-and-Orhan

d. Hughes, Thomas Patrick, "Ghazi". *Dictionary of Islam*, (W. H. Allen & Co., 1885)

e. Kokhar, Zain. "Osman I" (2020). *World History Encyclopedia.* https://www.worldhistory.org/Osman_I/

f. National Geographic, "The Silk Road", (2025). https://education.nationalgeographic.org/resource/silk-road/

g. Routly, Nick, "A Fascinating Map of Medieval Trade Routes" (May 24, 2018). *Visual Capitalist.* https://www.visualcapitalist.com/medieval-trade-route-map/#google_vignette

6. **BARBARY AND TURKISH "CORSAIRS" MAKE THE MEDITERRANEAN DANGEROUS FOR ITALIAN MERCHANTS.**

a. Davis, Robert C., *Christian Slaves, Muslim Masters,* (Palgrave MacMillan, 2003)

b. Dyson, John, *Columbus: For Gold, God and Glory,* (Simon and Schuster, 1991)

c. Khan, Syed Muhammad, "Battles and Conquests of the Ottoman Empire (1299-1683)" (2021), *World History Encyclopedia,* https://www.worldhistory.org/article/1791/battles--conquests-of-the-ottoman-empire-1299-1683/

7. **ITALIAN SEA CAPTAINS CROSS THE ATLANTIC. COLUMBUS FINDS AMERICA AND GREAT WEALTH FOR SPAIN.**

a. Barber, John and Howe, *Henry, Historical Collections of the State of New Jersey.* (B. Olds for J.H. Bradley, 1852). p. 9, Posted Online by Library of Congress

b. https://www.loc.gov/resource/gdcmassbookdig.historicalcollec00barber/?st=gallery

c. Biographies.net. *"Manuel Pessanha"*. (2025)

d. https://www.biographies.net/people/en/manuel_pessanha

e. Brittanica.com. *"Da Verrazano"* (2025)

f. https://www.britannica.com/biography/Giovanni-da-Verrazzano

g. Demetri, Justin. *"Great Italian Explorers"*. https://lifeinitaly.com/great-italian-explorers/

h. Dyson, John, *supra*

8. SPAIN FIGHTS COSTLY WARS AGAINST THE OTTOMAN TURKS AND THEIR BARBARY ALLIES

a. Drelichman, Mauricio and Voth, Hans-Joachim (2010), "The Sustainable Debts of Philip II", *Working Papers,* Centre de Recerca en Economia Internacional https://crei.cat/wp-content/uploads/users/working-papers/voth_sustainabledebts.pdf

b. Jennings, R. (1993). *Christians and Muslims in Ottoman Cyprus and the Mediterranean world, 1571-1640* (Vol. 1). NYU Press.

c. Korpas, Zoltan, (20220 "History Is Written by Victorious Battles: Glorious Lepanto (1571) and Forgotten Preveza (1538)", Turkish Journal of History, 76 (2022/1) 63-91

d. Libby, L. (1978), Venetian Views of the Ottoman Empire from the Peace of 1503 to the War of Cyprus, *Sixteenth Century Journal,* 9(4), 103. https://www.jstor.org/stable/2540047

e. Lumen Learning (2025) "Philip II and the Spanish Armada", *Western Civilization.* https://courses.lumenlearning.com/atd-herkimer-westerncivilization/chapter/philip-ii-and-the-spanish-armada/

f. McNeill, W.H., *The Rise of the West,* (The New American Library, 1963). pp. 676-677

g. New World Encyclopedia. *"Ottoman Habsburg Wars"* (2025). https://www.newworldencyclopedia.org/entry/Ottoman-Habsburg_wars

h. Rafferty, John P. "From Pirate to Admiral: The Tale of Barbarossa". (2025) *Britannica.*

i. Vella, Andrew P. "The Order of Malta and the Defense of Tripoli 1530-1551" (1969), *Libya in History: Historical Conference 1968* (Beirut-Lebanon, 1969) Republished by Library of Universitat Malta (2025). https://www.um.edu.mt/library/oar/bitstream/123456789/37478/1/3.pdf

9. SPAIN ALSO FIGHTS "WARS OF RELIGION" AGAINST PROTESTANT CHRISTIANS. ITS "ARMADA" FAILS TO SUBDUE ENGLAND.

a. Heath, Richard, "The Threat of the Ottoman Empire" (2025). *Emperor Charles V*, https://www.emperorcharlesv.com/charles-v-world/ottoman-empire-threat/

b. Jeon, Brian S., "Sixteenth-Century Spanish Fiscal Mismanagement and Debtor Emperors: An Economic History Review of Spain under Charles V in 1528 and under Philip II in 1575" (2014)

c. Luther, Martin, "19 Theses" (1517). Posten online by the Luther Memorial Foundation of Saxony-Anhalt. https://www.luther.de/en/95thesen.html

d. Musee Protestant. "The Eight Wars of Religion in Detail". (2025). *Musee Protestant.* https://museeprotestant.org/en/parcours/les-huit-guerres-de-religion/ and https://museeprotestant.org/en/notice/premiere-guerre-de-religion-1562-1563/?parc=36101

e. SpainThenAndNow.com. *"Charles V of Spain-Politics"* (2025). Site Currently Unavailable

f. Trim, David J.B. (2010). *"The Reformation and Wars of Religion"* (2010). Liberty Magazine https://www.libertymagazine.org/article/the-reformation-and-wars-of-religion

10. ENGLAND FAILS TO REACH CHINA WHEN IT SAILS NORTH AND WEST. ITS SETTLERS STARVE IN JAMESTOWN.

a. Bodenhemier, Lou. (2025). "Exploration Mysteries: A 16th-Century Arctic Expedition Ends in Disaster". *Explorers Web* https://explorersweb.com/exploration-mysteries-a-16th-century-arctic-expedition-ends-in-disaster/

b. Britannica.com. *"Muscovy Company"* (2025). https://www.britannica.com/topic/Muscovy-Company

c. Mariner's Museum. "Henry Hudson", 2025. https://exploration.marinersmuseum.org/subject/henry-hudson/

d. Price, David A. "Jamestown Colony". (2025). Britannica.com. https://www.britannica.com/place/Jamestown-Colony

e. Wolfe, Brendan, « Early Jamestown Settlement » (2025). Encyclopedia Virginia. https://encyclopediavirginia.org/entries/jamestown-settlement-early/

11. LAND, LIBERTY, AND SLAVES SAVE JAMESTOWN.

a. Boaz, James. "Private Property Saved Jamestown. And With It America" (2007). *Cato Institute.* https://www.cato.org/commentary/private-property-saved-jamestown-it-america

b. FunBarbadosHome. (2025). The History of Slavery in Barbados. https://www.funbarbados.com/ourisland/history/slavery.cfm?vm=r&s=1

c.   Handler, Jerome S. (2019). An Early Edict on Slavery in English America: The Barbados Resolution of 1636 and the Island's Slave Laws., Journal of the Barbados Museum & Historical Society.

d.   Mark, Joshua J, "Virginia Slave Laws and the Development of Colonial American Slavery" (9/24/2021), *Brewminate.com,* https://brewminate.com/virginia-slave-laws-and-the-development-of-colonial-american-slavery/

e.   Nicholson, Bradley J., "Legal Borrowing and the Origins of Slave Laws in the British Colonies" (1/1/1994), *American Journal of Legal History,* https://academic.oup.com/ajlh/article-abstract/38/1/38/1799003

f.   VirginiaPlaces.org. "How Colonists Acquired Title To Land in Virginia". (2025). http://www.itsuandi.org/itsui/downloads/Itsui_Materials/How-Colonists-Acquired-Title-to-Land-in-Virginia.pdf

g.   Wolfe, Brendan. "Indentured Servants in Colonial Virginia" *Encyclopedia Virginia. Virginia Humanities,* (07 Dec. 2020). Web. 01 Nov. 2025. Last updated: 2025, February 13

h.   https://encyclopediavirginia.org/entries/indentured-servants-in-colonial-virginia/

12. SLAVERY IS NORMAL IN MOST OF THE WORLD.

a.   Images:

  i.   "Arab Slave Trading Caravan" (c. 1860). Probably from Drawing by John Frederick Lewis. Wikipedia Commons. Public Domain in the United States.

  ii.   "Overview of the Slave Trade out of Africa, 1500-1900" *from Atlas of the Transatlantic Slave Trade,* David Eltis, David Richardson, (Yale University Press, 2010), https://www.jstor.org/stable/j.ctt5vm1s4. Used with permission of Yale University Press.

b.   Text:

  i.   Birmingham, David, Trade and Conflict in Angola, (Clarendon Press, 1966). Posted online by Internet Archive in 2020. https://archive.org/details/tradeconflictina0000birm/page/n5/mode/2up

  ii.   David Eltis, David Richardson, *Atlas of the Transatlantic Slave Trade,* (Yale University Press, 2010). pp 21-36 https://www.jstor.org/stable/j.ctt5vm1s4

  iii.   Davis, Robert C., *Christian Slaves, Muslim Masters: White Slavery in the Mediterranean, the Barbary Coast, and Italy, 1500-1800* (Palsgrave Macmillan, 2003)

  iv.   Lovejoy, Paul E., Transformation of Slavery in Africa 2d Ed., (Cambridge University Press, 2000), p 46, 47 and 142. https://archive.org/details/transformationsi0000love/page/142/mode/1up

v. Madany, Bassam Michael, "The Veiled Genocide: A Forgotten Historic Trage-dy" From Acorn to Oak, Level 12 (5/22/2018),https://fromacorntooak12.com/wp-content/uploads/2021/08/The_Veiled_Genocide_A_forgotten_Historic-1.pdf

vi. N'Diaye, Tidiane, *Genocide Voile (LE) (The Veiled Genocide)*, (Folio, 2017)

13. ENGLAND LETS "SEPARATISTS" RUN THEIR OWN CHURCHES IF THEY GO TO AMERICA.

a. Claveau, Victor, "Martyrs During the Protestant Reformation in England". (2025). *The Evangelization Station.* https://evangelizationstation.com/martyrs-during-the-prot-estant-reformation-in-england/

b. Dodgers, Rev. Anthony. "Robert Barnes, A Lutheran Martyr in England" (2017). *Lutheran Reformation.org* https://lutheranreformation.org/history/robert-barnes-lu-theran-martyr-england/

c. Foxe, John, *Fox's Book of Martyrs.* (1563). Republished Project Gutenberg (2025). https://www.gutenberg.org/cache/epub/22400/pg22400.txt

d. Klugewicz, Stephen M., "Founding Father: John Carroll & the Creation of the Catholic Church in America". (April 7th, 2024). *The Imaginative Conservative.* https://theimag-inativeconservative.org/2024/04/founding-father-john-carroll-creation-catho-lic-church-america-stephen-klugewicz.html

e. Plimoth Patuxet Museum, "Who Were the Pilgrims", (2025). https://plimoth.org/for-students/homework-help/who-were-the-pilgrims

f. Powell, K.J., *The Marian Martyrs and the Reformation in Bristol,* (Bristol Branch of the Historical Association, The University Bristol, 1972)

14. THE PILGRIMS STARVE WHEN "THE COMMUNITY" OWNS ALL LAND. THEY FEAST AND GIVE THANKS WHEN EACH FAMILY FARMS ITS OWN PARCEL.

a. Bethel, Tom. (1999). How Private Property Saved the Pilgrims. *Hoover Institution.*

b. Bradford, William, *Of Plimoth Plantation: From the Original Manuscript* (Boston: Wright and Potter, State Printers, 1898), pp. 162-164. Posted online by Project Gutenberg in 2019. https://www.gutenberg.org/files/24950/24950-h/24950-h.htm#a1623

c. General Society of Mayflower Descendents. "The Mayflower Compact", (2025), https://themayflowersociety.org/history/the-mayflower-compact/

d. Reed, Lawrence W. "Why the Pilgrims Abandoned Common Ownership for Private Property", (2024) *Foundation for Economic Education (FEE)*

15. THE DUTCH CONQUER AND SETTLE ALONG THE DELAWARE RIVER WHEN ENGLAND IS WEAK FROM CIVIL WARS.

a. Britannica. "English Civil Wars" (2025). https://en.wikipedia.org/wiki/English_Civil_War

b. Britannica. "Sir George Carteret, Baronet" (2025).

c. Hanson, Marilee. "The New Model Army" (1/17/2022), English History. https://englishhistory.net/stuarts/civil-war/the-new-model-army/

d. Historical Society of the New York Courts, "1621 Charter of the Dutch West India Company". (2025). https://history.nycourts.gov/about_period/charter-1621/

e. Lumen Learning, "The Dutch in America", U.S. History I (2025). https://courses.lumenlearning.com/wm-ushistory1/chapter/dutch-colonization/

f. Royal Family of the United Kingdom. "Charles I (r. 1625-1649)" (2025). https://www.royal.uk/charles-i

g. Royal Family of the United Kingdom. "James II (r. 1685-1688)". (2025), https://www.royal.uk/james-ii

h. The Twickenham Museum. "Lord John Berkeley 1607-1678". (2025). https://twickenham-museum.org.uk/people/warriors-and-wars/lord-john-berkeley/

16. PARLIAMENT UNITES ENGLAND. CHARLES II AND JAMES DRIVE OUT THE DUTCH AND CREATE NEW JERSEY.

a. Barber, John and Howe, *Henry, Historical Collections of the State of New Jersey.* (B. Olds for J.H. Bradley, 1852) p. 14 Posted Online by Library of Congress, https://www.loc.gov/resource/gdcmassbookdig.historicalcollec00barber/?st=gallery

b. Charles II, King of England to James, Duke of York, Patent Grant of Land in New England (March 8, 1664). America and West Indies: March 1664 | British History Online

c. "Concession and Agreement. . . of the Province of New Caesarea, or New Jersey. . ." (1664). The Avalon Project Yale Law School. https://avalon.law.yale.edu/17th_century/nj02.asp

d. Folsom, Joseph Fulford, et al. "Carteret, Philip". (1916) *Cyclopedia of New Jersey Biography.* Newark, N.J., Memorial history company, 1916. Pdf. Retrieved from the Library of Congress. Pp 3-6. #17 - Cyclopedia of New Jersey biography - Full View | HathiTrust Digital Library

e. Genealogical Society of Bergen County. (2014). "New Jersey at 350—A Short History of Colonial New Jersey Land Records". https://www.njgsbc.org/nj-colonial-land-records/

f. Goodspeed, Marfy, "How New Jersey Began" (1/26/2014), *Goodspeed Histories.* https://goodspeedhistories.com/how-new-jersey-began/

g. James, Duke of York, "Grant of New Jersey to John Berkely and George Carteret" (6/16/1664), NJ State Library, Thomas Edison State University. https://www.njstatelib.org/research_library/legal_resources/historical_laws/charters_and_treaties/the-grant-to-berkeley-and-carteret-1664/

h. Ogden, Evelyn H. (2016). *Founders of New Jersey.* Descendents of Founders of New Jersey. https://www.njfounders.org/book-by-evelyn-h-ogden-ed-d

i. Roper, L. H., "The Fall of New Netherland and Seventeenth-Century Anglo-American Imperial Formation, 1654-1676", *The New England Quarterly*, Vol. 87, No. 4 (December 2014), pp. 666-708 (43 pages) https://www.jstor.org/stable/43286385?read-now=1&seq=10#page_scan_tab_contents

j. Tondu, Gerard, "U.S. Timeline: 1665- 'Concession and Agreement' of New Jersey" (2025), https://gerard-tondu.blogspot.com/2016/03/1665-concession-and-agreement-of-new.html

k. Weslager, Charles A, The English on the Delaware, 1610-1682. 2nd, 1969 ed., (Rutgers University Press, 1967), 182 https://archive.org/details/englishondelawar0000wesl/page/180/mode/1up

l. Zeeuwarchief, "'Zeeuw' Conquers New York", (2025) *Zeews Archief,* https://www.zeeuwsarchief.nl/en/zeeland-stories/people-from-zeeland-all-over-the-world/zeeuw-verovert-new-york-in-1673/

17. GEORGE FOX STARTS THE "QUAKER" MOVEMENT IN ENGLAND. THOUSANDS OF HIS FOLLOWERS ARE PERSECUTED AND ARRESTED.

a. Brady, Marilyn Dell, "Early Quaker Families, 1650-1800", (2009), *Friends Journal*, Friends Publishing Company https://www.friendsjournal.org/2009060/

b. Fell, Margaret, "Chapter 19: Openings", *Quaker Faith and Practice.* (Yearly Meeting of the Religious Society of Friends (Quakers) in Britain, 2025) https://qfp.quaker.org.uk/chapter/19/

c. Fox, George *Journal of George Fox, 1624-1691* (1691) (Cambridge University Press, 1952) Internet Archive 1970. https://archive.org/details/journalofgeorgef00foxg/page/n5/mode/2up

d. McCormick, Richard P. (1964) *New Jersey from Colony to State: 1609-1789. Vol I. New Jersey Historical Series.* (Van Nostrand Co., 1964) pp. 38-39

e. Merriam-Webster, "Why Did We Stop Using 'Thou'". (2025) Merriam-Webster. https://www.merriam-webster.com/wordplay/why-did-we-stop-using-thou

f.   Padgett, Sally Bruyneel and Martinson, Donna, "Mother of Quakerism: Margaret Fell (1614-1702)", (2013) *Focus,* Intervarsity Christian Fellowship. https://thewell. intervarsity.org/focus/mother-quakerism-margaret-fell-1614-1702.html

g.   Pomfret, John E., *The Province of West New Jersey 1609-1702*, (Princeton University Press, 1956)

h.   Quakers in the World. "George Fox 1624-1691" (2025). https://www.quakersinthe-world.org/quakers-in-action/12/George-Fox

i.   Quinn, James. (undated). "William Penn. The Founding of the Quaker Colony of West Jersey". *Gwynedd Friends Meeting.* USHistory.org.https://www.ushistory. org/penn/pennnj.htm#google_vignette

j.   Tondu, Gerard E. L. "1672 Quaker Founder George Fox in America". (2016) Gerard-Tondu.blogspot.com. https://gerard-tondu.blogspot.com/2016/06/1672-quaker-founder-george-fox-in.html

k.   Watts, Alice, "Fearless Radicals Turned the Quakers from Advocates of Slavery to Fervent Abolitionists". (3/12/2021), HistoryNet, https://www.historynet.com/fearless--radicals-turned-the-quakers-from-advocates-of-slavery-to-fervent-abolitionists/

18. JURORS FIND WILLIAM PENN "NOT GUILTY" AND ARE SENT TO JAIL.

a.   "Case of Edward Bushel" (1670), *Internet Archive,* https://archive.org/details/bim_early-english-books-1641-1700_the-case-of-edward-bushe_bushell-edward_1670

b.   King Charles II, "A Proclamation Against All Meetings of Quakers, Anabaptists, &c."(1661), Oxford Text Archive, https://ota.bodleian.ox.ac.uk/repository/xmlui/bitstream/handle/20.500.12024/A92595/A92595.html?sequence=5

c.   Pierre, Clara, "In the Footsteps of William Penn" (February 1989), *Irish America Magazine,* https://www.irishamerica.com/2023/03/in-the-footsteps-of-william-penn/

d.   "The Tryal of William Penn & William Mead for Causing a Tumult, at the Sessions Held at the Old Bailey in London" (1670) Internet Archivd. https://archive.org/details/tryalofwilliampe0000unse_n7l4/page/16/mode/2up

19. QUAKERS BUY HALF OF NEW JERSEY

a.   Borough of Magnolia, NJ. "History" (2025). Borough of Magnolia, https://www.magnolia-nj.org/about/page/history

b.   Elmer, Lucius Q.C., "History of the Early Settlement and Progress of Cumberland County, by L.Q.C. Elmers, Chapter 1 (1869), (May 18, 2025). Posted online by West Jersey History Project. https://westjerseyhistory.org/books/Elmer/chapter1.shtml

c. Fox, George (1691). *supra,* Pages 1624-1691 https://archive.org/details/journalof-georgef00foxg/page/n5/mode/2up

d. Goodspeed, Marfy, "The Quaker George Fox". (2009) *Goodspeed Histories.* https://goodspeedhistories.com/the-quaker-george-fox/

e. Heston, Alfred. South Jersey, a History 1664-1924, Vol 11, (Lewis Historical Pub, 1937) p. 726, *Archive.org,* 1970.

f. Jones, Rufus M, Sharpless, Isaac, Gunmere Amelia M, *The Quakers in the American Colonies,* (Macmillan, 1911). P. 359 https://archive.org/details/quakersinamerica-00joneuoft/page/n14/mode/1up

g. Kelly, William E., *300 Years at the Point* (1994). Magic Image Productions, Inc., 1994) at Page 20

h. McCormick, Richard P., *supra,* pp. 43-45

i. Myers, Albert Cook, *Narratives of Early Pennsylvania, West New Jersey and Delaware 1630-1707.* (1912) Charles Scribner's Sons. P. 193

j. Penn, William (1677). "The Concessions and Agreements of the Proprietors. . . of West New-Jersey, in America, (1677)". *West Jersey.org.* (2025) https://westjersey.org/ca77.htm

k. Pomfret, John E., *supra,* pp. 65-70

l. Quakers in the World. "Mission Work and Quaker Settlement in Colonial New Jersey" (2025). https://www.quakersintheworld.org/quakers-in-action/280

m. Salmon, Erica. "50th Timeline: 1675 – Quakers Arrive in South Jersey". (2019) *Friends School Mullica Hill.* https://www.friendsmh.org/blog/50th-timeline-1675-quakers-arrive-in-southern-new-jersey/

n. United Kingdom Archives. (2025). "Currency Converter". https://www.nationalar-chives.gov.uk/currency-converter/#currency-result

o. Webster, Ian (2025). "UK Inflation Calculator". CPI *Inflation Calculator.* https://www.in2013dollars.com/uk/inflation/2017-to-2025

p. Wilson, Harold F. The Jersey Shore (Volume I) (Lewis Historical Publishing, 1953) Page 111

q. Wilson, Harold F. (1950). Outline History of New Jersey. (Rutgers University Press, 1950)

20. QUAKERS SETTLE IN SALEM AND BURLINGTON. WILLIAM PENN GIVES "WEST NEW JERSEY" A CONSTITUTION.

a. Borough of Magnolia, NJ. "History" (2025). Borough of Magnolia, https://www.magnolia-nj.org/about/page/history

b. "Concessions and Agreements. . . of West Jersey". (1677). WestJersey.org https://westjersey.org/ca77.htm

c. Elmer, Lucius Q.C., "History of the Early Settlement and Progress of Cumberland County, by L.Q.C. Elmers, Chapter 1 (1869), (May 18, 2025) https://westjerseyhistory.org/books/Elmer/chapter1.shtml

d. Fox, George (1691). *Journal of George Fox, supra*

e. Goodspeed, Marfy, "The Quaker George Fox". (2009) *Goodspeed Histories.* https://goodspeedhistories.com/the-quaker-george-fox/

f. Heston, Alfred. South Jersey, a History 1664-1924, Vol 11, (Lewis Historical Pub, 1937) p. 726, *Archive.org,* 1970.

g. Jones, Rufus M, Sharpless, Isaac, Gunmere Amelia M, *The Quakers in the American Colonies*, (Macmillan, 1911). P. 359 https://archive.org/details/quakersinamerica-00joneuoft/page/n14/mode/1up

h. McCormick, Richard P. (1964) *supra*

i. Penn, William (1677). "The Concessions and Agreements of the Proprietors. . . of West New-Jersey, in America, (1677)". *West Jersey.org.* (2025) https://westjersey.org/ca77.htm

j. Pomfret, John E., *The Province of West New Jersey 1609-1702*, (Princeton University Press, 1956) pp. 107-112

k. Quakers in the World. "Mission Work and Quaker Settlement in Colonial New Jersey" (2025). https://www.quakersintheworld.org/quakers-in-action/280

l. Salmon, Erica. "50th Timeline: 1675 – Quakers Arrive in South Jersey". (2019) *Friends School Mullica Hill.* https://www.friendsmh.org/blog/50th-timeline-1675-quakers-arrive-in-southern-new-jersey/

m. Sidney, Algernon, The arraignment, tryal & condemnation of Algernon Sidney, Esq. for high-treason ... before the Right Honourable Sir George Jeffreys ... Lord Chief Justice of England at His Majesties Court of Kingsbench at Westminster on the 7th, 21th and 27th of November, 1683 | Early English Books Online | University of Michigan Library Digital Collections

n. Smith, Samuel, *supra, at p. 95, 441. https://archive.org/details/bim_eighteenth-century_the-history-of-the-colon_smith-samuel_1765*

o. Wilson, Harold F., *The Jersey Shore* (Volume I) (Lewis Historical Publishing, 1953) Page 111

21. MOST LENNI-LENAPE LEAVE NEW JERSEY AND MOVE NORTH AND WEST.

a. Barber, John and Howe, *supra* at pp. 61-63.

b. Budd, Thomas, *Good Order Established in Pennsylvania and New Jersey in America* (Original Published in London, *1685). pp 65-66, 70-72 https://archive.org/stream/ goodorderestabli00thom/goodorderestabli00thom_djvu.txt*

c. Cohler, Max. "New Jersey Natives: The Lenni Lenape" 2015. *South Jersey.com* https:// www.southjersey.com/articles/?articleid=21055 https://quod.lib.umich.edu/e/evans/ N06429.0001.001/1:2?rgn=div1;view=fulltext

d. Thomas, Gabriel *supra* at p. 13

e. Quakers In the World. "Mission Work and Quaker Settlement in Colonial New Jersey" (2025). https://www.quakersintheworld.org/quakers-in-action/280/Mission-work-and-Quaker-settlement-in-colonial-New-Jersey

f. Smith, Samuel, *supra* pp 440, 441.

g. "The Minutes of a treaty held at Easton, in Pennsylvania, in October, 1758, etc." https:// name.umdl.umich.edu/N06429.0001.001. University of Michigan Library Digital Collections. Accessed December 1, 2025.

h. Waugaman, David, "The Great Easton Treaty of 1758" (2017) Department of History, Graduate School of Wichita State University. https://soar.wichita.edu/server/api/core/ bitstreams/9b27b40e-f712-49d2-82b2-25ef85f37498/content

i. Webb, Scott, "The Penn Family and Pennsylvania Colony" (5/27/2024), *The History of Silver,* https://historyofsilverlake.com/the-penn-family-and-pennsylvania-colony/

22. AMERICANS BREAK TREATY OF EASTON. A LENAPE PREACHER INSPIRES "PONTIAC'S WAR".

a. Burke, Peter and Pratt, Adam, "Native Resistance to Conversion – Native History of the Wyoming Valley". (2022). University of Scranton. https://digitalprojects.scranton.edu/s/native-history-wyoming-valley/page/native-resistance-to-conversion

b. Burton, Clarence Monroe, Digital History, "The Proclamation of 1763" (2025). University of Houston. https://www.digitalhistory.uh.edu/disp_textbook.cfm?smtID=3&psid=159

c. Hunter, Charles E., "The Delaware Nativist Revival of the Mid-Eighteenth Century" (Winter, 1971), Ethnohistory, Duke University Press. https://www.jstor.org/ stable/481593?read-now=1

d. King George III, "Proclamation of October 7, 1763". Printed by Mark Baskett, Printer to the King's Most Excellent Majesty, Posted online by Gilder Lehrman Collection. https://www.gilderlehrman.org/sites/default/files/inline-pdfs/t-05214.pdf

e. Navarre, Robert, *Journal of Pontiac's Conspiracy-1763,* (Clarence Monroe Burton/ Speaker Hines Printing Company, 1912) https://babel.hathitrust.org/cgi/pt?id=yal e.39002032938731&seq=10

23. JOHN SOMERS BUILDS A LOG HOUSE NEAR THE "POINT" WHERE THE RIVER MEETS THE GREAT EGG HARBOR.

a. Findagrave.com. "John Somers (1648-1723)" (2025). https://www.findagrave.com/memorial/24080426/john-somers

b. Kelly, William E., *supra*, Pages 20-26.

c. Longislandsurnames.com. John Somers: 1648-1723 https://longislandsurnames.com/getperson.php?personID=I08370&tree=Williams

d. Wikitree. "John Somers (1648-1723)". (2025) https://www.wikitree.com/wiki/Somers-8

24. SOMERS AND HIS NEIGHBORS ENJOY PROSPEROUS AND COMFORTABLE LIVES

a. Kelly, William E., *supra,* Pages 29-30.

b. Thomas, Gabriel. *Historical and Geographical Account of Pennsylvania and West New Jersey.* (A Baldwin, 1698) https://www.si.edu/object/account-pennsylvania-and-west-new-jersey-gabriel-thomas-reprinted-original-edition-1698-introduction:siris_sil_1106641

c. Thomas, Gabriel. Pennsylvania, "Poor Man's Paradise " (1698) https://minnstate.pressbooks.pub/ushistory1/chapter/poor-mans-paradise-1698/

25. DANIEL COX APPLIES HIS "CURIOUS" MIND TO SCIENCE, MEDICINE, AND BUSINESS.

a. Find a Grave, "Col. Daniel Coxe" (2025). https://www.findagrave.com/memorial/232740073/daniel-coxe

b. Fox, Karen. "Whalers: The Link To Our Past" (2009), Cape May.com. https://www.capemay.com/blog/2009/11/whalers-the-link-to-our-past/

c. Goodspeed, Marfy, "Daniel Cox, Merchant Investor" (5/27/2010), https://goodspeedhistories.com/daniel-coxe-merchant-investor/, "Daniel Coxe, Scientist and Politician" (4/8/2010), https://goodspeedhistories.com/more-on-the-curious-dr-daniel-coxe/, "The 'Inquisitive' Dr. Coxe" (4/14/2010), https://goodspeedhistories.com/the-inquisitive-dr-coxe/ The Learned and Intelligent Dr. Coxe" (4/20/2010), https://goodspeedhistories.com/the-learned-and-intelligent-dr-daniel-coxe/

d. Hunter, Michael, "Royal Society" (2025) *Britannica.* https://www.britannica.com/topic/Royal-Society

e. Pepys, Samuel, "Diary Entry of May 3, 1665", *Diary of Samuel Pepys* 1660-1669, https://www.pepysdiary.com/diary/1665/05/

f. Pomfret, John E., *supra*

g. Ronkowitz, Ken. "Whaling in Historic New Jersey". (2012). https://endangerednj.
    blogspot.com/2012/09/whaling-in-historic-new-jersey.html

h. Royal Society, "A Further Relation of the Whale-Fishing about the Bermudas,
    and on the Coast of New-England and New Netherland" (1665-1678). https://ar-
    chive.org/details/philtrans08605038/mode/1u

26. DANIEL COXE'S RELIGION AND POLITICS ARE DANGEROUS IN ENGLAND, BUT WELCOME IN NEW JERSEY.

a. Image: Farr, David, "John Blackwell and Daniel Cox: Further Notes on Their Activi-
    ties in Restoration England and British North America." *The Pennsylvania Magazine
    of History and Biography*, vol. 123, no. 3 (Jul., 1999), pp. 227-233. https://journals.psu.
    edu/pmhb/article/view/45311/45032

b. Goodspeed, Marfy, "Daniel Coxe, Merchant Investor" (5/27/2010), https://good-
    speedhistories.com/daniel-coxe-merchant-investor/Daniel Coxe, Scientist and Pol-
    itician" (4/8/2010), https://goodspeedhistories.com/more-on-the-curious-dr-dan-
    iel-coxe/ "The Inquisitive Dr. Cox" (4/14/2010), https://goodspeedhistories.com/
    the-inquisitive-dr-coxe/ "The Radical Daniel Coxe" (4/22/2010), *Goodspeed Histories.*
    https://goodspeedhistories.com/the-radical-daniel-coxe/

c. King Charles II, "A Proclamation Against Tumultous Petitions" (1679), https://quod.
    lib.umich.edu/e/eebo/A32361.0001.001/1:1?rgn=div1;view=fulltext

d. Wigfield, W. MacDonald, *The Monmouth Rebellion: a social history, including the com-
    plete text of Wade's Narrative, 1685*, (Barnes and Noble Books, 1980).

27. DANIEL COXE OWNS A MILLION ACRES OF LAND IN WEST NEW JERSEY.

a. Find a Grave, "Col. Daniel Coxe" (2025). https://www.findagrave.com/memori-
    al/232740073/daniel-coxe

b. Goodspeed, Marfy, "Daniel Coxe, Merchant Investor" (5/27/2010), https://good-
    speedhistories.com/daniel-coxe-merchant-investor/, "West New Jersey", https://
    goodspeedhistories.com/west-new-jersey-1674-1680/, Coxe's Landholdings, 1688,
    https://goodspeedhistories.com/coxes-landholdings-1688/, "West NJ 1688 & Daniel
    Coxe", https://goodspeedhistories.com/west-nj-1688-and-daniel-coxe-part-1/

c. Hunter, Michael, "Royal Society" (2025) *Britannica.* https://www.britannica.com/
    topic/Royal-Society

d. Pomfret, John E., *supra*

28. DANIEL COXE BUILDS "WHALE FISHING", POTTERY AND SHIP-BUILDING INDUSTRIES IN WEST NEW JERSEY WITHOUT LEAVING ENGLAND.

a. Find a Grave, "Col. Daniel Coxe" (2025). https://www.findagrave.com/memorial/232740073/daniel-coxe

b. Fox, Karen. "Whalers: The Link To Our Past" (2009), Cape May.com. https://www.capemay.com/blog/2009/11/whalers-the-link-to-our-past/

c. Goodspeed, Marfy, "1688, Daniel Coxe's Schemes" (7/31/2010), https://goodspeed-histories.com/1688-daniel-coxes-schemes/, "The Early Years of West New Jersey", "Regarding Dr. Daniel Coxe", Goodspeed Histories (2009-2010) "West NJ 1688 & Daniel Coxe" (7/24/2010), https://goodspeedhistories.com/west-nj-1688-and-daniel-coxe-part-1/

d. Heston, *Alfred M, supra* at p. 531.

e. Hunter, Michael, "Royal Society" (2025) *Britannica.* https://www.britannica.com/topic/Royal-Society

f. Pomfret, John E., *supra*

g. Ronkowitz, Ken. "Whaling in Historic New Jersey". (2012). https://endangerednj.blogspot.com/2012/09/whaling-in-historic-new-jersey.html

h. Royal Society, "A Further Relation of the Whale-Fishing about the Bermudas, and on the Coast of New-England and New Netherland" (1665-1678). https://archive.org/details/philtrans08605038/mode/1u

i. Taylor, D. Joshua, "Past But Not Forgotten: North Carolina's Jersey Settlement" (2020), North Carolina Geneaology. https://www.ncgenealogy.org/wp-content/uploads/public/vc_handouts_2020/Past_But_Not_Forgotten-Taylor.pdf

j. Xiao, Zhao, "Market Economies With Churches and Market Economies Without Churches". (2002). Paper explained in interview "FRONTLINE/World. Jesus in China Interview/PBS". (7/24/2008). https://www.pbs.org/frontlineworld/stories/china_705/interview/xiao.html

29. JOHN TOWNSEND COMES FOR FREEDOM. MOST LONG ISLAND WHALERS COME TO CAPE MAY FOR LAND.

a. Dorwart, Jeffery M., *Cape May County, New Jersey,* (Rutgers University Press, 1993). p 19

b. Fox, Karen. "Whalers: The Link To Our Past" (2009), Cape May.com. https://www.capemay.com/blog/2009/11/whalers-the-link-to-our-past/

c. Geni.com. "John Townsend of Cape May 1658-1721" (2025). https://www.geni.com/people/John-Townsend-of-Cape-May/6000000034612464858

d. Reeves, Randall R. and Mitchell, Edward, "Shore Whaling for Right Whales in the Northeastern United States", Final Report, (U.S. Department of Commerce, NOAA, National Marine Fisheries Service, 1987) https://www.yumpu.com/en/document/read/13384798/shore-whaltng-f-northeast-fisheries-science-center-noaa/44

e. Romm, Richard M., "America's First Whaling Industry And The Whaler Yeomen Of Cape May 1630-1830", Thesis, Graduate School Rutgers Camden, (2010) State University of New Jersey. https://rucore.libraries.rutgers.edu/rutgers-lib/27287/

f. Ronkowitz, Ken. "Whaling in Historic New Jersey". (2012). https://endangerednj.blogspot.com/2012/09/whaling-in-historic-new-jersey.html

g. Stevens, Lewis Townsend. *History of Cape May County.* (Heritage Books, 2011).

h. TheShoreBlog.com. "History of Townsend's Inlet" (2017). https://theshoreblog.com/history-of-townsends-inlet/

i. Townsend Society of America. "The Townsend Family of Long Island" (2025). https://longislandgenealogy.com/Surname_Pages/townsend.htm

j. Walsh, Anne, "Historic Town Bank, New Jersey: A Timeline" (2025). *Cape May Magazine.* https://www.capemaymag.com/feature/historic-town-bank-new-jersey-a-timeline/

k. Wikipedia. "John Townsend (Oyster Bay)" (2025). https://en.wikipedia.org/wiki/John_Townsend_(Oyster_Bay)

l. Wikitree. "John Townsend" (2025). https://www.wikitree.com/wiki/Townsend-39

30. RICHARD SOMERS REPLACES HIS FATHER'S LOG HOUSE WITH A BRICK "MANSION".

a. AutoBrik Magazine. (Unknown). "Making Brick in the Playground of the World"

b. Ewan, Nat. R. (1970). "Early Brickmaking in the Colonies". (1970) West Jersey History Project. https://www.westjerseyhistory.org/articles/brickmaking/

c. Kelly, William. (1994) *supra*, at pp.25, 31

d. Miller, Diane Jr. , "What Caused a Quaker Boy to Become an Armed Soldier in the American Revolution." *Atlantic County Historical Society Newsletter,* October, 2025. From ACHS Geneology Folder 221A, p. 250.

31. JAMES SOMERS BUILDS A DAM AND TWO MILLS. HE KEEPS HIS BARGAIN IN BARGAINTOWN.

a. Kelly, William, *supra,*

b. Mason, Beryl D. "Bargaintown" (1964) Sketches of Egg Harbor Township. Egg Harbor Twp Tercentenary Committee. http://bdweb7057k.bluedomino.com/history/Sketches/bargaintown/index.htm

c. Myers, Albert Cook (1912) *Narratives of Early Pennsylvania, West Jersey and Delaware: 1630-1707.* (Charles Scribner's Sons, 1912).

32. PENNSYLVANIA AND WEST NEW JERSEY "ARE VERY GREAT AND INVITING FOR POOR PEOPLE".

a. Goodspeed, Marfy. (2010). "West Jersey, 1690 Part One". *Goodspeed Histories,* https://goodspeedhistories.com/west-new-jersey-1690-part-one/

b. Johnson, Paul (1997) *History of the American People.* (Harper Collins, 1997) p95

c. Smith, Samuel, supra, pp *67, 111-112*

d. Thomas, Gabriel. "Pennsylvania, the Poor Man's Paradise", (1698), *supra*

33. QUAKERS BUY AND OWN BLACK AFRICANS AS SLAVES IN SOUTH JERSEY AND PENNSYLVANIA.

a. Cadbury, Henry J., *John Hepburn and his Book against Slavery,* (Davis Press, Inc., 1949) Posted Online. Docslib.org (2025) https://docslib.org/doc/8600685/john-hepburn-and-his-book-against-slavery-1715

b. Dorwart, Jeffery M., *Cape May County, New Jersey*, (Rutgers University Press, 1993). p 39

c. Fox, George *Journal of George Fox, 1624-1691* (1691) (Cambridge University Press, 1952) Internet Archive 1970. pp. 598-599, 604. https://archive.org/details/journalofgeorgef00foxg/page/n5/mode/2up

d. Galenson, David W. (1980). "Demographic Aspects of White Servitude in Colonial British America". (1980) Editions Belen https://www.persee.fr/doc/adh_0066-2062_1980_num_1980_1_1466

e. Hepburn, John, *The American Defense of the Christian Golden Rule,* (John Hepburn, 1714), Posted online by Internet Archive in 2025. https://archive.org/details/bim_eighteenth-century_the-american-defence-of-_hepburn-john_1715/mode/2up Keyser, Richard, "Chapter 3.0 Indentured Servants: Introduction". (2020) *American Legal History to the 1860s.* University of Wisconsin. https://wisc.pb.unizin.org/ls261/chapter/b-indentured-servitude-in-the-colonies/

f. Quakers in the World. "Mission Work and Quaker Settlement in Colonial New Jersey" (2025). https://www.quakersintheworld.org/quakers-in-action/280

g. Watts, Alice, "Fearless Radicals Turned the Quakers from Advocates of Slavery to Fervent Abolitionists". (3/12/2021), HistoryNet, https://www.historynet.com/fearless-radicals-turned-the-quakers-from-advocates-of-slavery-to-fervent-abolitionists/

h. Woolman, John, *The Works of John Woolson: In Two Parts,* (Printed by Joseph Cruk-shank, 1774), Posted Online by https://digital.librarycompany.org/islandora/object/Islandora%3A48100?solr_nav%5Bid%5D=df7e8301b7054938d947&solr_nav%5Bpage%5D=0&solr_nav%5Boffset%5D=44#page/8/mode/1up

34. A BURLINGTON QUAKER IS INDICTED FOR "GIVING BLOWS" TO A "NEGRO SERVANT WOMAN" THAT "OCCASIONED HER DEATH." A JURY FINDS HIM "NOT GUILTY".

a. Goodspeed, Marfa, "Death of a Negro Servant" (11/23/2010) *Goodspeed Histories,* https://goodspeedhistories.com/the-death-of-a-negro-woman-servant/

b. Reed, H. Clay and Miller, George Julius, The Burlington Court Book, A Record of Quaker Jurisprudence in West New Jersey, 1680-1709, (American Historical Association, 1974) pp. 56-57 https://archive.org/details/burlingtoncourtb00unse/page/57/mode/1up

35. AFTER THIRTY YEARS, A FEW QUAKERS DEMAND FREEDOM FOR BLACK SLAVES.

a. Galenson, David W. (1980). "Demographic Aspects of White Servitude in Colonial British America". (1980) Editions Belen, https://www.persee.fr/doc/adh_0066-2062_1980_num_1980_1_1466

b. Hepburn, John, *supra*

c. Koedel, R. Craig. "Chapter 8: The Fight Against Slavery", *South Jersey Heritage.* (University Press of America, 1979) https://westjersey.org/sjh/sjh_chap_8.htm

d. Rediker, Marcus, "The 'Quaker Comet' Was the Greatest Abolitionist You Never Heard Of". (Sep 2017). *Smithsonian Magazine.* https://www.smithsonianmag.com/history/quaker-comet-greatest-abolitionist-never-heard-180964401/

e. Rosenbloom, Joshua. (2023). "Indentured Servitude in the Colonial U.S." (2023) *Economic History Association.* https://eh.net/encyclopedia/indentured-servitude-in-the-colonial-u-s/

36. A TAILOR FROM MOUNT HOLLY SHAMES QUAKERS INTO FREEING THEIR SLAVES.

a. Hack, Timothy. (undated). Transcribed Documents of the New Jersey Society for Promoting the Abolition of Slavery. West Jersey History Project. https://westjerseyhistory.org/docs/timhack/

b. Johnson, Paul. A History of the American People. (Harper Collins, 1997).

c. Koedel, R. Craig. "Chapter 8: The Fight Against Slavery", *South Jersey Heritage*. (University Press of America, 1979) https://westjersey.org/sjh/sjh_chap_8.htm

d. Rosenbloom, Joshua. (2023). "Indentured Servitude in the Colonial U.S." (2023) *Economic History Association.* https://eh.net/encyclopedia/indentured-servitude-in-the-colonial-u-s/

e. Toler, Christopher, "Gouldtown: A Cumberland County Locale Rooted in Afro-Indian History, Geneology" (6/22/2021), *SNJ Today,* https://snjtoday.com/gouldtown-a-cumberland-county-locale-rooted-in-afro-indian-history-genealogy/

f. Wolfe, Brendan. "Indentured Servants in Colonial Virginia" *Encyclopedia Virginia.* Virginia Humanities, (07 Dec. 2020). Web. 10 Nov. 2025. P.53, https://encyclopediavirginia.org/entries/indentured-servants-in-colonial-virginia.

g. Woolman, John, *supra*

37. SHIPS ARE BUILT, AND IRON IS FORGED THROUGHOUT SOUTH JERSEY.

a. Gambrell, Debbie and Cayley, Michael, "Mahlon Stacy Sr. (1638 - 1704)" (2025), Wikitree, https://www.wikitree.com/wiki/Stacy-192

b. Koedel, R. Craig. "Chapter 10. From Ships to Soup", (1979). *South Jersey Heritage,* University Press of America, and Shipbuilding: An Early Shore Industry, (Publication S2081 of the Atlantic County Historical Society, 1986). Pp. 100-101

c. McCormick, Richard P., *supra*, at p. 53.

d. Pierce, Arthur D. *Iron in the Pines.* (Rutgers University Press, 1957)

e. Smith, Samuel, supra at pp 67, *111-112,*

38. NEW JERSEY GOVERNMENT IS "EXTREMELY SMALL, LIMITED IN ITS POWERS, AND CHEAP."

a. Barber, John and Howe, Henry, *supra*, at p 24

b. Reed, H. Clay and Miller, George J., *Burlington Court Book of West New Jersey 1680-1709. (American Historical Society, 1944).* Posted online by Archive.org at https://archive.org/details/burlingtoncourtb00unse

c. Johnson, Paul. *A History of the American People.* (Harper Collins, 1997) Page 108

d. Murphy, Gov. Philip, "Governor Murphy Signs Legislation to Eliminate the Title of 'Freeholder' from Public Office". *Office of the Governor Media Release.* (August 21, 2020) https://www.nj.gov/governor/news/news/562020/20200821b.shtml

e. New Jersey League of Municipalities. "Origins of the Property Tax in New Jersey". (2025). https://www.njlm.org/1354/Origins-of-the-Property-Tax-in-New-Jerse

f. New Jersey State Constitution of 1776. https://www.nj.gov/state/archives/docconst76.html

g. Zablocki, Peter, How Women in New Jersey Gained—and Lost—the Right to Vote More Than a Century Before the 19th Amendment Granted Suffrage Nationwide, Smithsonian Magazine (July 8, 2025) https://www.smithsonianmag.com/history/how-women-in-new-jersey-gained-and-lostthe-right-to-vote-more-than-a-century--before-the-19th-amendment-granted-suffrage-nationwide-180986930/?utm_source=copilot.com

39. FEW CHILDREN GO TO PUBLIC SCHOOLS, BUT MOST LEARN "THE THREE R'S."

a. Budd, Thomas, *Good Order Established in Pennsylvania and New Jersey in America* (Original Published in London, *1685).* https://archive.org/stream/goodorderestabli00thom/goodorderestabli00thom_djvu.txt

b. Burr, Nelson R., *Education in New Jersey: 1630-1871,* (Princeton University Press, 1942) p. 367

c. Franklin, Benjamin. (1791). *The Autobiography of Benjamin Franklin of 1791.* Chartwell Books. P. 115. https://www.gutenberg.org/files/20203/20203-h/20203-h.htm

d. Kull, Irving, *New Jersey- a History Volume I,* (American Historical Society, Inc., 1930). Pp 371

e. Reed, H. Clay and Miller, George J., *Burlington Court Book of West New Jersey 1680-1709. (American Historical Society, 1944).* Posted online by Archive.org at https://archive.org/details/burlingtoncourtb00unse

40. SUCCESS AND TOLERANCE MAKE QUAKERS A MINORITY IN THEIR OWN "HOMELAND."

a. Duffin, J.M. and Hagedorn, Nancy R., "Philadelphia in 1775" (2025), 'Revolution at Penn?' Exhibition, *Penn Libraries*, University of Pennsylvania. https://storymaps.arcgis.com/stories/42a8107416c94c5cbfd92ded2050dbff

b. Johnson, Paul, *supra* at pp 108-109

c. Kashatus, William C., Philadelphia Quakers: A Brief History (2009)

d. Linder, Douglas O. "The Life, Trials and Execution of Mary Dyer: An Account", *Famous Trials*, (University of Missouri-Kansas City Law School, 2019). https://famous-trials.com/dyer/2489-the-life-trials-and-execution-of-mary-dyer-an-account

e.   National Humanities Center, Primary Resources in U.S. History er. "Cities and Towns: Growth, Becoming American: The British Atlantic Colonies 1690-1763" (2009). *Primary Resources in U.S. History and Literature. Toolbox Library,* National Humanities Center. https://nationalhumanitiescenter.org/pds/becomingamer/growth/text2/text2read.htm

f.   Pomfret, John E., *supra* at pp 493-519,

g.   Rhode Island Heritage Hall of Fame. "Mary (Barrett) Dyer" (2025). https://riheritagehalloffame.com/mary-dyer/

41. AMERICANS HAVE A "GREAT AWAKENING" OF CHRISTIAN FAITH.

a.   Belcher, Joseph, *George Whitefield, a Biography,* (American Tract Society, 1857) pp.16, 18 Posted online by Archive.org. https://ia803400.us.archive.org/13/items/georgewhitefield0000belc_u3r7/georgewhitefield0000belc_u3r7.pdf

b.   Clark, D. "Child mortality in the U.S 1800-2020". *Statista.com* (2025). https://www.statista.com/statistics/1041693/united-states-all-time-child-mortality-rate/

c.   Villegas, Teresa, "Before Modern Medicine, What Proportion of Women Died During Childbirth?" (2025), How We Became a Family, https://howwebecameafamily.com/before-modern-medicine-what-proportion-of-women-died-during-childbirth.html

d.   Fairchild, Mary, "George Whitefield, Spellbinding Evangelist of the Great Awakening". (2019). *Learning Religions.* https://www.learnreligions.com/george-whitefield-4689110

e.   Franklin, Benjamin. (1791), supra "George Whitefield".

f.   Heyrman, Christine Leigh, "The First Great Awakening, Divining America" *TeacherServe.* (2025). National Humanities Center. https://nationalhumanitiescenter.org/tserve/eighteen/ekeyinfo/grawaken.htm

g.   Kidd, Thomas, "The Science of Sound: Whitefield's Massive Crowds" (2014). *The Gospel Coalition.*

h.   https://www.thegospelcoalition.org/article/the-science-of-sound-whitefields-massive-crowds/

i.   Olson, Mark. "George Whitefield's Doctrine of Conversion – 1735-1740" Wesley Scholar. com https://wesleyscholar.com/george-whitefields-doctrine-of-conversion-1735-1740/

j.   Revival Library, "William Tennent Sr. 1673-1746-Leader in the Great Awakening". *The Revival Library* https://revival-library.org/william-tennent/

k.   Woolman, John, *The Works of John Woolman: In Two Parts,* (Printed by Joseph Crukshank, 1774), Posted Online by Digital Library Company (2025)

42. GEORGE WHITEFIELD AWAKENS PHILADELPHIA AND SOUTH JERSEY.

a. Koedel, Craig, God's Vine in this Wilderness, (Gloucester County Historical Society, 1980) pp. 45-46

b. Palmer, F. Alan, "The Presbyterian Parish of Deerfield Street", History & Cemetery of Deerfield Presbyterian Church, (2025) https://deerfieldpres.org/history/

43. QUAKERS ARE ALSO AWAKENED, AND FREE MORE SLAVES.

a. Bradley, Clara. "Black History Month-History of Lawnside, NJ". *Town Crier-Legislative Backgrounder.* (2023*).* NJ League of Municipalities. https://www.njlm.org/Blog.aspx?IID=218

b. Diemer, Andrew. "Free Black Communities". *Encyclopedia of Greater Philadelphia.* (2017 https://philadelphiaencyclopedia.org/essays/free-black-communities/

c. "Fairfield Presbyterian Old Stone Church" (2025), *Exploring Cumberland County,* Cumberland County Cultural and Historical Commission.

d. Koedel, Craig, God's Vine in this Wilderness, (Gloucester County Historical Society, 1980) pp. 69-81

e. Cumberland County Department of Planning, Tourism and Community Affairs, "Fairfield Presbyterian Old Stone Church" (2025), Explore Cumberland NJ, https://explorecumberlandnj.com/cumberland-historic-sites/fairfield-presbyterian-old-stone-church/

f. "Trinity African Methodist Episcopal Church" (2025), *Explore Cumberland County,* Cumberland County Cultural and Historical Society. https://explorecumberlandnj.com/cumberland-historic-sites/trinity-african-methodist-episcopal-church/

g. Woolman, John, *supra*

44. SOUTH JERSEY BECOMES PART OF A NEW AMERICAN NATION.

a. Clark, Elmer T., "The Journal and Letters of Francis Asbury", (2025). *Wesley Center Online.* Northwest Nazarene University.

b. Johnson, Paul, *supra at p 95*

c. Stanger, Frank Bateman. *The Methodist Trail in New Jersey. (New Jersey Annual Conferences of Methodis, 1961) pp 69, 80, 97, 99, 102, 145.*

Appendix of Original Sources

- Barber, John and Howe, *Henry, Historical Collections of the State of New Jersey.* (B. Olds for J.H. Bradley, 1852). https://www.loc.gov/resource/gdcmassbookdig.historicalcollec00barber/?st=gallery

- Bradford, William, *Of Plimoth Plantation: From the Original Manuscript* (Boston: Wright and Potter, State Printers, 1898), pp. 162-164. Posted online by Project Gutenberg in 2019. https://www.gutenberg.org/files/24950/24950-h/24950-h.htm#a1623

- Budd, Thomas, *Good Order Established in Pennsylvania and New Jersey in America* (Original Published in London, *1685). https://archive.org/stream/goodorderestabli00thom/goodorderestabli00thom_djvu.txt*

- "Case of Edward Bushel" (1670), *Internet Archive*, https://archive.org/details/bim_early-english-books-1641-1700_the-case-of-edward-bushe_bushell-edward_1670

- Charles II, King of England to James, Duke of York, Patent Grant of Land in New England (March 8, 1664). America and West Indies: March 1664 | British History Online

- *Clark, Elmer T.,* "The Journal and Letters of Francis Asbury", (2025). *Wesley Center Online.* Northwest Nazarene University.

- "Concession and Agreement. . . of the Province of New Caesarea, or New Jersey. . ." (1664). The Avalon Project Yale Law School. https://avalon.law.yale.edu/17th_century/nj02.asp

- "Concessions and Agreements. . . of West Jersey". (1677). WestJersey.org https://westjersey.org/ca77.htm

- Fox, George *Journal of George Fox, 1624-1691* (1691) (Cambridge University Press, 1952) Internet Archive 1970. https://archive.org/details/journalofgeorgef00foxg/page/n5/mode/2up

- Franklin, Benjamin. (1791). "George Whitefield". *The Autobiography of Benjamin Franklin of 1791.* Chartwell Books. P. 115. https://www.gutenberg.org/files/20203/20203-h/20203-h.htm

- 'Germantown Friends Protest against Slavery" (1688). Posted online by National Park Service at https://www.nps.gov/articles/000/inde-germantown-friends-protest-slavery-1688.htm

- Hack, Timothy. (undated). Transcribed Documents of the New Jersey Society for Promoting the Abolition of Slavery. West Jersey History Project. https://westjerseyhistory.org/docs/timhack/

- Harriott, Thomas. "A Briefe and True Report of the New Found Land of Virginia" (1588). Part 3. Posted online by U.S. National Park Service at https://nps.gov/fora/learn/education/the-third-and-last-part.htm

- Hepburn, John, *The American Defense of the Christian Golden Rule,* (John Hepburn, 1714), Posted online by Internet Archive in 2025. https://archive.org/details/bim_eighteenth-century_the-american-defence-of-_hepburn-john_1715/mode/2up

- James, Duke of York, "Grant of New Jersey to John Berkely and George Carteret" (6/16/1664), NJ State Library, Thomas Edison State University. https://www.njstatelib.org/research_library/legal_resources/historical_laws/charters_and_treaties/the-grant-to-berkeley-and-carteret-1664/

- King Charles II, "A Proclamation Against All Meetings of Quakers, Anabaptists, &c."(1661), Oxford Text Archive, https://ota.bodleian.ox.ac.uk/repository/xmlui/bitstream/handle/20.500.12024/A92595/A92595.html?sequence=5

- King Charles II, "A Proclamation Against Tumultous Petitions" (1679), https://quod.lib.umich.edu/e/eebo/A32361.0001.001/1:1?rgn=div1;view=fulltext

- King George III, "Proclamation of October 7, 1763". Printed by Mark Baskett, Printer to the King's Most Excellent Majesty, Posted online by Gilder Lehrman Collection.

- Luther, Martin, "19 Theses" (1517). Posten online by the Luther Memorial Foundation of Saxony-Anhalt. https://www.luther.de/en/95thesen.html

- Murphy, Gov. Phil. "Governor Murphy Signs Legislation to Eliminate the Title of 'Freeholder' from Public Office". *Office of the Governor Media Release.* (August 21, 2020). https://www.nj.gov/governor/news/news/562020/20200821b.shtml

- Navarre, Robert, Journal of Pontiac's Conspiracy-1763, (Clarence Monroe Burton/Speaker Hines Printing Company, 1912) https://babel.hathitrust.org/cgi/pt?id=yale.39002032938731&seq=10

- Pepys, Samuel, "Diary Entry of May 3, 1665", *Diary of Samuel Pepys* 1660-1669, https://www.pepysdiary.com/diary/1665/05/

- Reed, H. Clay and Miller, George Julius, The Burlington Court Book, A Record of Quaker Jurisprudence in West New Jersey, 1680-1709, (American Historical Association, 1974) pp. 56-57 https://archive.org/details/burlingtoncourtb00unse/page/57/mode/1up

- Royal Society, "A Further Relation of the Whale-Fishing about the Bermudas, and on the Coast of New-England and New Netherland" (1665-1678). https://archive.org/details/philtrans08605038/mode/1up

- Sidney, Algernon (1683). The arraignment, tryal & condemnation of Algernon Sidney, Esq. for high-treason ... before the Right Honourable Sir George Jeffreys ... Lord Chief Justice of England at His Majesties Court of Kingsbench at Westminster on the 7th, 21th and 27th of November, 1683 | Early English Books Online | University of Michigan Library Digital Collections

- Smith, Samuel (1765). *The History of the Colony of Nova-Cæsaria, or New-Jersey, etc. (WS Sharp, 1877) pp67, https://archive.org/details/bim_eighteenth-century_the-history-of-the-colon_smith-samuel_1765*

- Treaty of Easton. "The Minutes of a treaty held at Easton, in Pennsylvania, in October, 1758, etc." https://name.umdl.umich.edu/N06429.0001.001. University of Michigan Library Digital Collections. Accessed December 1, 2025.

- Thomas, Gabriel. *Historical and Geographical Account of Pennsylvania and West New Jersey.* (A Baldwin, 1698) https://www.si.edu/object/account-pennsylvania-and-west-new-jersey-gabriel-thomas-reprinted-original-edition-1698-introduction:siris_sil_1106641

- "Tryal of William Penn & William Mead for Causing a Tumult, at the Sessions Held at the Old Bailey in London" (1670) *Internet Archive.* https://archive.org/details/tryalofwilliampe0000unse_n7l4/page/16/mode/2up

- Wigfield, W. MacDonald, *The Monmouth Rebellion: a social history, including the complete text of Wade's Narrative, 1685*, (Barnes and Noble Books, 1980)

- Woolman, John, *The Works of John Woolman: In Two Parts,* (Printed by Joseph Crukshank, 1774), Posted Online by https://digital.librarycompany.org/islandora/object/Islandora%3A48100?solr_nav%5Bid%5D=df7e8301b7054938d947&solr_nav%5Bpage%5D=0&solr_nav%5Boffset%5D=44#page/8/mode/1up (2025)